MznLnx

Missing Links Exam Preps

Exam Prep for

International Economics

Sawyer, Sprinkle, 2nd Edition

The MznLnx Exam Prep is your link from the texbook and lecture to your exams.
The MznLnx Exam Preps are unauthorized and comprehensive reviews of your textbooks.

All material provided by MznLnx and Rico Publications (c) 2010
Textbook publishers and textbook authors do not particpate in or contribute to these reviews.

MznLnx

Rico
Publications

Exam Prep for International Economics
2nd Edition
Sawyer, Sprinkle

Publisher: Raymond Houge
Assistant Editor: Michael Rouger
Text and Cover Designer: Lisa Buckner
Marketing Manager: Sara Swagger
Project Manager, Editorial Production: Jerry Emerson
Art Director: Vernon Lowerui

Product Manager: Dave Mason
Editorial Assitant: Rachel Guzmanji
Pedagogy: Debra Long
Cover Image: Jim Reed/Getty Images
Text and Cover Printer: City Printing, Inc.
Compositor: Media Mix, Inc.

(c) 2010 Rico Publications
ALL RIGHTS RESERVED. No part of this work
covered by the copyright may be reproduced or
used in any form or by an means--graphic, electronic,
or mechanical, including photocopying, recording,
taping, Web distribution, information storage, and
retrieval systems, or in any other manner--without the
written permission of the publisher.

Printed in the United States
ISBN:

For more information about our products, contact us at:
Dave.Mason@RicoPublications.com

For permission to use material from this text or
product, submit a request online to:
Dave.Mason@RicoPublications.com

Contents

CHAPTER 1
Introduction: An Overview of the World Economy — 1

CHAPTER 2
Why Countries Trade — 7

CHAPTER 3
Factor Endowments and the Commodity Composition of Trade — 14

CHAPTER 4
Intraindustry Trade — 22

CHAPTER 5
International Factor Movements — 26

CHAPTER 6
Tariffs — 30

CHAPTER 7
Nontariff Distortions to Trade — 32

CHAPTER 8
International Trade Policy — 36

CHAPTER 9
Regional Economic Arrangements — 41

CHAPTER 10
International Trade and Economic Growth — 46

CHAPTER 11
National Income Accounting and the Balance of Payments — 52

CHAPTER 12
International Transactions and Financial Markets — 57

CHAPTER 13
Exchange Rates and Their Determination: A Basic Model — 62

CHAPTER 14
Money, Interest Rates, and the Exchange Rate — 65

CHAPTER 15
Price Levels and Exchange Rates in the Long Run — 70

CHAPTER 16
Output and the Exchange Rate in the Short Run — 75

CHAPTER 17
Macroeconomic Policy and Floating Exchange Rates — 81

CHAPTER 18
Fixed Exchange Rates and Currency Unions — 87

CHAPTER 19
International Monetary Arrangements — 94

CHAPTER 20
Capital Flows and the Developing Countries — 99

ANSWER KEY — 102

TO THE STUDENT

COMPREHENSIVE

The *MznLnx* Exam Prep series is designed to help you pass your exams. Editors at MznLnx review your textbooks and then prepare these practice exams to help you master the textbook material. Unlike study guides, workbooks, and practice tests provided by the texbook publisher and textbook authors, *MznLnx* gives you **all** of the material in each chapter in exam form, not just samples, so you can be sure to nail your exam.

MECHANICAL

The MznLnx Exam Prep series creates exams that will help you learn the subject matter as well as test you on your understanding. Each question is designed to help you master the concept. Just working through the exams, you gain an understanding of the subject--its a simple mechanical process that produces success.

INTEGRATED STUDY GUIDE AND REVIEW

MznLnx is not just a set of exams designed to test you, its also a comprehensive review of the subject content. Each exam question is also a review of the concept, making sure that you will get the answer correct without having to go to other sources of material. You learn as you go! Its the easiest way to pass an exam.

HUMOR

Studying can be tedious and dry. MznLnx's instructional design includes moderate humor within the exam questions on occassion, to break the tedium and revitalize the brain

Chapter 1. Introduction: An Overview of the World Economy

1. _____s is the social science that studies the production, distribution, and consumption of goods and services. The term _____s comes from the Ancient Greek οἰκονομῐ́α from οἶκος (oikos, 'house') + νόμος (nomos, 'custom' or 'law'), hence 'rules of the house(hold)'. Current _____ models developed out of the broader field of political economy in the late 19th century, owing to a desire to use an empirical approach more akin to the physical sciences.
   - a. Energy economics
   - b. Inflation
   - c. Opportunity cost
   - d. Economic

2. _____ is a branch of economics with three main subdisciplines international trade, monetary economics and international finance.

   - International trade studies goods-and-services flows across international boundaries from supply-and-demand factors, economic integration, and policy variables such as tariff rates and trade quotas.
   - International finance studies the flow of capital across international financial markets, and the effects of these movements on exchange rates.
   - International monetary economics and macroeconomics studies money and macro flows across countries.
   - Stanley W. Black (2008.) 'international monetary institutions,' The New Palgrave Dictionary of Economics. 2nd Edition.

   - a. Index number
   - b. International economics
   - c. Economic depreciation
   - d. ACCRA Cost of Living Index

3. _____ is a branch of economics that deals with the performance, structure, and behavior of a national or regional economy as a whole. Along with microeconomics, _____ is one of the two most general fields in economics. It is the study of the behavior and decision-making of entire economies.
   - a. Nominal value
   - b. New Trade Theory
   - c. Tobit model
   - d. Macroeconomics

4. _____ is a branch of economics that studies how individuals, households and firms and some states make decisions to allocate limited resources, typically in markets where goods or services are being bought and sold. _____ examines how these decisions and behaviours affect the supply and demand for goods and services, which determines prices; and how prices, in turn, determine the supply and demand of goods and services.

   Whereas macroeconomics involves the 'sum total of economic activity, dealing with the issues of growth, inflation and unemployment, and with national economic policies relating to these issues' and the effects of government actions on them.

   - a. Countercyclical
   - b. New Keynesian economics
   - c. Recession
   - d. Microeconomics

5. The _____ or gross domestic income (GDI), a basic measure of an economy's economic performance, is the market value of all final goods and services produced within the borders of a nation in a year. _____ can be defined in three ways, all of which are conceptually identical. First, it is equal to the total expenditures for all final goods and services produced within the country in a stipulated period of time (usually a 365-day year.)
   - a. Countercyclical
   - b. Monopolistic competition
   - c. Market structure
   - d. Gross domestic product

Chapter 1. Introduction: An Overview of the World Economy

6. The _____ is an international financial institution that provides financial and technical assistance to developing countries for development programs (e.g. bridges, roads, schools, etc.) with the stated goal of reducing poverty.

The _____ differs from the _____ Group, in that the _____ comprises only two institutions:

- International Bank for Reconstruction and Development (IBRD)
- International Development Association (IDA)

Whereas the latter incorporates these two in addition to three more:

- International Finance Corporation (IFC)
- Multilateral Investment Guarantee Agency (MIGA)
- International Centre for Settlement of Investment Disputes (ICSID)

John Maynard Keynes (right) represented the UK at the conference, and Harry Dexter White represented the US.

The _____ is one of two major financial institutions created as a result of the Bretton Woods Conference in 1944. The International Monetary Fund, a related but separate institution, is the second.

a. World Bank
b. Flow to Equity-Approach
c. Bank-State-Branch
d. Financial costs of the 2003 Iraq War

7. In economics, _____ is the total demand for final goods and services in the economy (Y) at a given time and price level. It is the amount of goods and services in the economy that will be purchased at all possible price levels. This is the demand for the gross domestic product of a country when inventory levels are static.

a. Aggregate expenditure
b. Aggregation problem
c. Aggregate supply
d. Aggregate demand

8. Economics:

- _____, the desire to own something and the ability to pay for it
- _____ curve, a graphic representation of a _____ schedule
- _____ deposit, the money in checking accounts
- _____ pull theory, the theory that inflation occurs when _____ for goods and services exceeds existing supplies
- _____ schedule, a table that lists the quantity of a good a person will buy it each different price
- _____ side economics, the school of economics at believes government spending and tax cuts open economy by raising _____

a. McKesson ' Robbins scandal
b. Demand
c. Variability
d. Production

9. _____ is a misspelled phrase from Latin 'pro capite' phrase meaning per head with pro meaning 'per' or 'for each' and capite meaning 'head.' Both words together equate to the phrase 'for each head.'

Chapter 1. Introduction: An Overview of the World Economy

It is usually used in the field of statistics to indicate the average per person for any given concern, such as income, crime rate, etc.

It is also used in wills to indicate that each of the named beneficiaries should receive, by devise or bequest, equal shares of the estate. This is in contrast to a per stirpes division, in which each branch of the inheriting family inherits an equal share of the estate.

a. Population statistics
b. Per capita
c. False positive rate
d. Sargan test

10. In economics, an _____ is any good or commodity, transported from one country to another country in a legitimate fashion, typically for use in trade. _____ goods or services are provided to foreign consumers by domestic producers. _____ is an important part of international trade.
a. ACEA agreement
b. AD-IA Model
c. ACCRA Cost of Living Index
d. Export

11. In economics, an _____ is any good (e.g. a commodity) or service brought into one country from another country in a legitimate fashion, typically for use in trade. It is a good that is brought in from another country for sale. _____ goods or services are provided to domestic consumers by foreign producers. An _____ in the receiving country is an export to the sending country.
a. Economic integration
b. Incoterms
c. Import
d. Import quota

12. _____ or human capital flight is a large emigration of individuals with technical skills or knowledge, normally due to conflict, lack of opportunity, political instability, or health risks. _____ is usually regarded as an economic cost, since emigrants usually take with them the fraction of value of their training sponsored by the government. It is a parallel of capital flight which refers to the same movement of financial capital.
a. 130-30 fund
b. 100-year flood
c. 1921 recession
d. Brain drain

13. A _____ is an object whose consumption increases the utility of the consumer, for which the quantity demanded exceeds the quantity supplied at zero price. _____s are usually modeled as having diminishing marginal utility. The first individual purchase has high utility; the second has less.
a. Pie method
b. Composite good
c. Merit good
d. Good

14. _____ is a measurement of the economic output of a state or province. It is the sum of all value added by industries within the state and serves as a counterpart to the gross domestic product or GDP.

Conceptually, there is no difficulty in taking the definition of GDP for a nation and applying it to a smaller jurisdiction such as a state, or even a local government area.

a. Capital consumption allowance
b. Water footprint
c. Purchasing power parity
d. Gross State Product

Chapter 1. Introduction: An Overview of the World Economy

15. The _____ is a treaty of the World Trade Organization (WTO) that entered into force in January 1995 as a result of the Uruguay Round negotiations. The treaty was created to extend the multilateral trading system to service sector, in the same way the General Agreement on Tariffs and Trade (GATT) provides such a system for merchandise trade.

All members of the WTO are signatories to the GATS.

a. GATT
b. General Agreement on Trade in Services
c. General Agreement on Tariffs and Trade
d. Dutch-Scandinavian Economic Pact

16. _____ in its classic form is defined as a company from one country making a physical investment into building a factory in another country. It is the establishment of an enterprise by a foreigner. Its definition can be extended to include investments made to acquire lasting interest in enterprises operating outside of the economy of the investor.

a. Financial Stability Forum
b. Federal Deposit Insurance Corporation
c. Non-governmental organization
d. Foreign Direct Investment

17. A _____ or transnational corporation is a corporation or enterprise that manages production or delivers services in more than one country. It can also be referred to as an international corporation.

The first modern MNC is generally thought to be the Dutch East India Company, established in 1602.

a. Foreign direct investment
b. Luxembourg Income Study
c. Multinational corporation
d. Rakon

18. The _____ consists of a number of economic theories which describe the nature of the firm, company including its existence, its behaviour, and its relationship with the market.

In simplified terms, the _____ aims to answer these questions:

1. Existence - why do firms emerge, why are not all transactions in the economy mediated over the market?
2. Boundaries - why the boundary between firms and the market is located exactly there? Which transactions are performed internally and which are negotiated on the market?
3. Organization - why are firms structured in such specific way? What is the interplay of formal and informal relationships?

Despite looking simple, these questions are not answered by the established economic theory, which usually views firms as given, and treats them as black boxes without any internal structure.

The First World War period saw a change of emphasis in economic theory away from industry-level analysis which mainly included analysing markets to analysis at the level of the firm, as it became increasingly clear that perfect competition was no longer an adequate model of how firms behaved. Economic theory till then had focussed on trying to understand markets alone and there had been little study on understanding why firms or organisations exist.

Chapter 1. Introduction: An Overview of the World Economy

a. Policy Ineffectiveness Proposition
b. Technology gap
c. Khazzoom-Brookes postulate
d. Theory of the firm

19. In finance, the _____s between two currencies specifies how much one currency is worth in terms of the other. It is the value of a foreign nation;s currency in terms of the home nation;s currency. For example an _____ of 102 Japanese yen to the United States dollar means that JPY 102 is worth the same as USD 1.
    a. ACCRA Cost of Living Index
    b. ACEA agreement
    c. Interbank market
    d. Exchange rate

20. The _____ is where currency trading takes place. It is where banks and other official institutions facilitate the buying and selling of foreign currencies. FX transactions typically involve one party purchasing a quantity of one currency in exchange for paying a quantity of another.
    a. Floating currency
    b. Currency swap
    c. Covered interest arbitrage
    d. Foreign exchange market

21. The _____ is the broad group of people in contemporary society who fall socioeconomically between the working class and upper class. This socioeconomic class encompasses the sub-classes of lower middle, middle middle, and upper middle, and includes professionals, highly skilled workers, and management. As in all socioeconomic classes, the _____ is associated with a shared and complex set of cultural values.
    a. Dominant minority
    b. 100-year flood
    c. 130-30 fund
    d. Middle class

22. _____ in its literal sense is the process of transformation of local or regional phenomena into global ones. It can be described as a process by which the people of the world are unified into a single society and function together.

This process is a combination of economic, technological, sociocultural and political forces.

    a. Global Cosmopolitanism
    b. Globally Integrated Enterprise
    c. Helsinki Process on Globalisation and Democracy
    d. Globalization

23. _____ is the change in population over time, and can be quantified as the change in the number of individuals in a population using 'per unit time' for measurement. The term _____ can technically refer to any species, but almost always refers to humans, and it is often used informally for the more specific demographic term _____ rate , and is often used to refer specifically to the growth of the population of the world.

Simple models of _____ include the Malthusian Growth Model and the logistic model.

    a. 100-year flood
    b. Population dynamics
    c. Population growth
    d. 130-30 fund

24. _____ is money accepted for exchange of goods in an economy. The prevalence of one money over another arises, usually, when a government designates through decrees that the government shall accept only particular notes and coins in payment for taxes. Typically, money of _____ consists of stamped coins and minted paper bills.
    a. Security thread
    b. Local currency
    c. Currency
    d. Totnes pound

25. A _____ is a monetary authority which is required to maintain a fixed exchange rate with a foreign currency. This policy objective requires the conventional objectives of a central bank to be subordinated to the exchange rate target.

The main qualities of an orthodox _____ are:

- A _____'s foreign currency reserves must be sufficient to ensure that all holders of its notes and coins (and all banks creditor of a Reserve Account at the _____) can convert them into the reserve currency (usually 110-115% of the monetary base M0.)
- A _____ maintains absolute, unlimited convertibility between its notes and coins and the currency against which they are pegged (the anchor currency), at a fixed rate of exchange, with no restrictions on current-account or capital-account transactions.
- A _____ only earns profit from interests on foreign reserves (less the expense of note-issuing), and does not engage in forward-exchange transactions. These foreign reserves exist (1) because local notes have been issued in exchange, or (2) because commercial banks must by regulation deposit a minimum reserve at the _____. (1) generates a seignorage revenue. (2) is the revenue on minimum reserves (revenue of investment activities less cost of minimum reserves remuneration)
- A _____ has no discretionary powers to effect monetary policy and does not lend to the government. Governments cannot print money, and can only tax or borrow to meet their spending commitments.
- A _____ does not act as a lender of last resort to commercial banks, and does not regulate reserve requirements.
- A _____ does not attempt to manipulate interest rates by establishing a discount rate like a central bank. The peg with the foreign currency tends to keep interest rates and inflation very closely aligned to those in the country against whose currency the peg is fixed.

The _____ in question will no longer issue fiat money but instead will only issue one unit of local currency for each unit (or decided amount) of foreign currency it has in its vault (often a hard currency such as the U.S. dollar or the euro.) The surplus on the balance of payments of that country is reflected by higher deposits local banks hold at the central bank as well as (initially) higher deposits of the (net) exporting firms at their local banks.

a. Petrodollar
b. Currency competition
c. Reserve currency
d. Currency board

Chapter 2. Why Countries Trade

1. _____ was a survey conducted by the U.S. Department of Justice to gauge the prevalence of alcohol and illegal drug use among prior arrestees. It was a reformulation of the prior Drug Use Forecasting (DUF) program, focused on five drugs in particular: cocaine, marijuana, methamphetamine, opiates, and PCP.

Participants were randomly selected from arrest records in major metropolitan areas; because no personally identifying information is taken from each record chosen, the resulting data can be correlated to arrest rates, but not to the total population of persons charged.

   a. AD-IA Model
   b. Arrestee Drug Abuse Monitoring
   c. ACEA agreement
   d. ACCRA Cost of Living Index

2. _____ was a Scottish moral philosopher and a pioneer of political economy. One of the key figures of the Scottish Enlightenment, Smith is the author of The Theory of Moral Sentiments and An Inquiry into the Nature and Causes of the Wealth of Nations. The latter, usually abbreviated as The Wealth of Nations, is considered his magnum opus and the first modern work of economics.
   a. Adam Smith
   b. Adolf Hitler
   c. Alan Greenspan
   d. Adolph Fischer

3. In economics, _____ refers to the ability of a party to produce a good or service using fewer real resources than another entity producing the same good or service..A party has an _____ when using the same input as another party, it can produce a greater output. Since _____ is determined by a simple comparison of labor productivities, it is possible for a a party to have no _____ in anything. It can be contrasted with the concept of comparative advantage which refers to the ability to produce a particular good at a lower opportunity cost.
   a. ACCRA Cost of Living Index
   b. International economics
   c. Index number
   d. Absolute advantage

4. The concept was first developed in game theory and consequently zero-sum situations are often called _____s though this does not imply that the concept applies only to what are commonly referred to as games.

For 2-player finite _____s, the different game theoretic Solution concepts of Nash equilibrium, minimax, and maximin all give the same solution. In the solution, players play a mixed strategy.

   a. General purpose technologies
   b. Cash or share options
   c. Zero-sum game
   d. Gordon growth model

5. _____ is an economic theory that holds that the prosperity of a nation is dependent upon its supply of capital, and that the global volume of international trade is 'unchangeable.' Economic assets or capital, are represented by bullion (gold, silver, and trade value) held by the state, which is best increased through a positive balance of trade with other nations (exports minus imports.) _____ suggests that the ruling government should advance these goals by playing a protectionist role in the economy; by encouraging exports and discouraging imports, notably through the use of tariffs and subsidies.

_____ was the dominant school of thought throughout the early modern period (from the 16th to the 18th century.)

a. Consumer theory
b. General equilibrium theory
c. Nominal value
d. Mercantilism

6. _____, 1st Baron Keynes was a renowned economist from Britain whose many ideas on economic and political theories as well as on many governments' monetary policies influenced America. He advocated a government that played an active role in the lives of people regarding business, economy, etc. In this role, the government would use fiscal measures to reduce the consequences of recessions, economic depressions and booms.
   a. Adolf Hitler
   b. Adolph Fischer
   c. Adam Smith
   d. John Maynard Keynes

7. In microeconomics, _____ is quite simply the conversion of inputs into outputs. It is an economic process that uses resources to create a good or service that is suitable for exchange. This can include manufacturing, storing, shipping, and packaging.
   a. Production
   b. Red Guards
   c. Solved
   d. MET

8. _____ is the a method of technical and economic research of the systems for purpose to optimize a parity between system's consumer functions or properties and expenses to achieve those functions or properties.

This methodology for continuous perfection of production, industrial technologies, organizational structures was developed by Juryj Sobolev in 1948 at the 'Perm telephone factory'

- 1948 Juryj Sobolev - the first success in application of a method analysis at the 'Perm telephone factory'.
- 1949 - the first application for the invention as result of use of the new method.

Today in economically developed countries practically each enterprise or the company use methodology of the kind of functional-cost analysis as a practice of the quality management, most full satisfying to principles of standards of series ISO 9000.

- Interest of consumer not in products itself, but the advantage which it will receive from its usage.
- The consumer aspires to reduce his expenses
- Functions needed by consumer can be executed in the various ways, and, hence, with various efficiency and expenses. Among possible alternatives of realization of functions exist such in which the parity of quality and the price is the optimal for the consumer.

The goal of _____ is achievement of the highest consumer satisfaction of production at simultaneous decrease in all kinds of industrial expenses Classical _____ has three English synonyms - Value Engineering, Value Management, Value Analysis.

   a. Staple financing
   b. Monopoly wage
   c. Willingness to pay
   d. Function cost analysis

Chapter 2. Why Countries Trade

9. In economics, _____ refers to the ability of a person or a country to produce a particular good at a lower marginal cost and opportunity cost than another person or country. It is the ability to produce a product most efficiently given all the other products that could be produced. It can be contrasted with absolute advantage which refers to the ability of a person or a country to produce a particular good at a lower absolute cost than another.
   a. Gravity model of trade
   b. Hot money
   c. Triffin dilemma
   d. Comparative advantage

10. _____ is money accepted for exchange of goods in an economy. The prevalence of one money over another arises, usually, when a government designates through decrees that the government shall accept only particular notes and coins in payment for taxes. Typically, money of _____ consists of stamped coins and minted paper bills.
    a. Security thread
    b. Local currency
    c. Totnes pound
    d. Currency

11. A _____ is a monetary authority which is required to maintain a fixed exchange rate with a foreign currency. This policy objective requires the conventional objectives of a central bank to be subordinated to the exchange rate target.

The main qualities of an orthodox _____ are:

- A _____'s foreign currency reserves must be sufficient to ensure that all holders of its notes and coins (and all banks creditor of a Reserve Account at the _____) can convert them into the reserve currency (usually 110-115% of the monetary base M0.)
- A _____ maintains absolute, unlimited convertibility between its notes and coins and the currency against which they are pegged (the anchor currency), at a fixed rate of exchange, with no restrictions on current-account or capital-account transactions.
- A _____ only earns profit from interests on foreign reserves (less the expense of note-issuing), and does not engage in forward-exchange transactions. These foreign reserves exist (1) because local notes have been issued in exchange, or (2) because commercial banks must by regulation deposit a minimum reserve at the _____. (1) generates a seignorage revenue. (2) is the revenue on minimum reserves (revenue of investment activities less cost of minimum reserves remuneration)
- A _____ has no discretionary powers to effect monetary policy and does not lend to the government. Governments cannot print money, and can only tax or borrow to meet their spending commitments.
- A _____ does not act as a lender of last resort to commercial banks, and does not regulate reserve requirements.
- A _____ does not attempt to manipulate interest rates by establishing a discount rate like a central bank. The peg with the foreign currency tends to keep interest rates and inflation very closely aligned to those in the country against whose currency the peg is fixed.

The _____ in question will no longer issue fiat money but instead will only issue one unit of local currency for each unit (or decided amount) of foreign currency it has in its vault (often a hard currency such as the U.S. dollar or the euro.) The surplus on the balance of payments of that country is reflected by higher deposits local banks hold at the central bank as well as (initially) higher deposits of the (net) exporting firms at their local banks.

   a. Currency competition
   b. Petrodollar
   c. Reserve currency
   d. Currency board

Chapter 2. Why Countries Trade

12. Economics:
    - _____, the desire to own something and the ability to pay for it
    - _____ curve, a graphic representation of a _____ schedule
    - _____ deposit, the money in checking accounts
    - _____ pull theory, the theory that inflation occurs when _____ for goods and services exceeds existing supplies
    - _____ schedule, a table that lists the quantity of a good a person will buy it each different price
    - _____ side economics, the school of economics at believes government spending and tax cuts open economy by raising _____

    a. McKesson ' Robbins scandal
    c. Variability
    b. Production
    d. Demand

13. _____ s is the social science that studies the production, distribution, and consumption of goods and services. The term _____ s comes from the Ancient Greek οἰκονομία from οἶκος (oikos, 'house') + νόμος (nomos, 'custom' or 'law'), hence 'rules of the house(hold)'. Current _____ models developed out of the broader field of political economy in the late 19th century, owing to a desire to use an empirical approach more akin to the physical sciences.

    a. Opportunity cost
    c. Energy economics
    b. Inflation
    d. Economic

14. In economics, an _____ is any good or commodity, transported from one country to another country in a legitimate fashion, typically for use in trade. _____ goods or services are provided to foreign consumers by domestic producers. _____ is an important part of international trade.

    a. ACEA agreement
    c. AD-IA Model
    b. Export
    d. ACCRA Cost of Living Index

15. In economics, an _____ is any good (e.g. a commodity) or service brought into one country from another country in a legitimate fashion, typically for use in trade. It is a good that is brought in from another country for sale. _____ goods or services are provided to domestic consumers by foreign producers. An _____ in the receiving country is an export to the sending country.

    a. Incoterms
    c. Import quota
    b. Economic integration
    d. Import

16. _____ is a Regional Trade Agreement among Argentina, Brazil, Paraguay and Uruguay founded in 1991 by the Treaty of Asunción, which was later amended and updated by the 1994 Treaty of Ouro Preto. Its purpose is to promote free trade and the fluid movement of goods, people, and currency.

    _____ origins trace back to 1985 when Presidents Raúl Alfonsín of Argentina and José Sarney of Brazil signed the Argentina-Brazil Integration and Economics Cooperation Program or PICE.

    a. Free trade area
    c. 100-year flood
    b. 130-30 fund
    d. MERCOSUR

Chapter 2. Why Countries Trade

17. The _____ is a trilateral trade bloc in North America created by the governments of the United States, Canada, and Mexico. The agreement creating the trade bloc came into force on January 1, 1994. It superseded the Canada-United States Free Trade Agreement between the U.S. and Canada.
    a. Demand-side technologies
    b. Federal Reserve Bank Notes
    c. Case-Shiller Home Price Indices
    d. North American Free Trade Agreement

18. _____ in economics refers to metrics and measures of output from production processes, per unit of input. Labor _____, for example, is typically measured as a ratio of output per labor-hour, an input. _____ may be conceived of as a metrics of the technical or engineering efficiency of production.
    a. Fordism
    b. Production-possibility frontier
    c. Piece work
    d. Productivity

19. A _____ is an expression that compares quantities relative to each other. The most common examples involve two quantities, but any number of quantities can be compared. _____s are represented mathematically by separating each quantity with a colon, for example the _____ 2:3, which is read as the _____ 'two to three'.
    a. 100-year flood
    b. Ratio
    c. Y-intercept
    d. 130-30 fund

20. The slope of the production-possibility frontier (PPF) at any given point is called the _____ It describes numerically the rate at which one good can be transformed into the other. It is also called the (marginal) 'opportunity cost' of a commodity, that is, it is the opportunity cost of X in terms of Y at the margin.
    a. Productivity
    b. Piece work
    c. Fordism
    d. Marginal rate of transformation

21. _____ or economic opportunity loss is the value of the next best alternative foregone as the result of making a decision. _____ analysis is an important part of a company's decision-making processes but is not treated as an actual cost in any financial statement. The next best thing that a person can engage in is referred to as the _____ of doing the best thing and ignoring the next best thing to be done.
    a. Industrial organization
    b. Economic
    c. Economic ideology
    d. Opportunity cost

22. An _____ is an economy that is self-sufficient and does not take part in international trade, or severely limits trade with the outside world. Likewise the term refers to an ecosystem not affected by influences from the outside, which relies entirely on its own resources. In the economic meaning, it is also referred to as a closed economy.
    a. Autarky
    b. Underground economy
    c. Internet Economy
    d. Attention work

23. In international economics and international trade, _____ or _____ is the relative prices of a country's export to import. '_____' are sometimes used as a proxy for the relative social welfare of a country, but this heuristic is technically questionable and should be used with extreme caution. An improvement in a nation's _____ is good for that country in the sense that it has to pay less for the products it import.
    a. Terms of trade
    b. Kennedy Round
    c. Common market
    d. Commercial invoice

24. The '_____' is approximately the nominal interest rate minus the inflation rate Since the inflation rate over the course of a loan is not known initially, volatility in inflation represents a risk to both the lender and the borrower.

In economics and finance, an individual who lends money for repayment at a later point in time expects to be compensated for the time value of money, or not having the use of that money while it is lent.

a. Core inflation
b. Reflation
c. Cost-push inflation
d. Real interest rate

25. A _____ is something for which there is demand, but which is supplied without qualitative differentiation across a market. It is a product that is the same no matter who produces it, such as petroleum, notebook paper, or milk. In other words, copper is copper.

a. Soft commodity
b. 100-year flood
c. Hard commodity
d. Commodity

26. _____ is a fee paid on borrowed assets. It is the price paid for the use of borrowed money, or, money earned by deposited funds. Assets that are sometimes lent with _____ include money, shares, consumer goods through hire purchase, major assets such as aircraft, and even entire factories in finance lease arrangements.

a. Internal debt
b. Interest
c. Insolvency
d. Asset protection

27. An _____ is the price a borrower pays for the use of money they do not own, for instance a small company might borrow from a bank to kick start their business, and the return a lender receives for deferring the use of funds, by lending it to the borrower. _____s are normally expressed as a percentage rate over the period of one year.

_____s targets are also a vital tool of monetary policy and are used to control variables like investment, inflation, and unemployment.

a. Enterprise value
b. Interest rate
c. ACCRA Cost of Living Index
d. Arrow-Debreu model

28. The _____ or gross domestic income (GDI), a basic measure of an economy's economic performance, is the market value of all final goods and services produced within the borders of a nation in a year. _____ can be defined in three ways, all of which are conceptually identical. First, it is equal to the total expenditures for all final goods and services produced within the country in a stipulated period of time (usually a 365-day year.)

a. Monopolistic competition
b. Market structure
c. Gross domestic product
d. Countercyclical

29. _____ is a misspelled phrase from Latin 'pro capite' phrase meaning per head with pro meaning 'per' or 'for each' and capite meaning 'head.' Both words together equate to the phrase 'for each head.'

It is usually used in the field of statistics to indicate the average per person for any given concern, such as income, crime rate, etc.

It is also used in wills to indicate that each of the named beneficiaries should receive, by devise or bequest, equal shares of the estate. This is in contrast to a per stirpes division, in which each branch of the inheriting family inherits an equal share of the estate.

Chapter 2. Why Countries Trade

a. False positive rate
b. Sargan test
c. Population statistics
d. Per capita

30. In calculus, a function f defined on a subset of the real numbers with real values is called _____, if for all x and y such that x >≤ y one has f(x) >≤ f(y), so f preserves the order. In layman's terms, the sign of the slope is always positive (the curve tending upwards) or zero (i.e., non-decreasing, or asymptotic, or depicted as a horizontal, flat line) Likewise, a function is called monotonically decreasing (non-increasing) if, whenever x >≤ y, then f(x) >≥ f(y), so it reverses the order.

a. 1921 recession
b. 130-30 fund
c. 100-year flood
d. Monotonic

31. In microeconomic theory, an _____ is a graph showing different bundles of goods, each measured as to quantity, between which a consumer is indifferent. That is, at each point on the curve, the consumer has no preference for one bundle over another. In other words, they are all equally preferred.

a. Indifference curve
b. Expenditure minimization problem
c. Indifference map
d. Engel curve

32. In economics, the _____ is the rate at which a consumer is ready to give up one good in exchange for another good while maintaining the same level of satisfaction.

Under the standard assumption of neoclassical economics that goods and services are continuously divisible, the marginal rates of substitution will be the same regardless of the direction of exchange, and will correspond to the slope of an indifference curve (more precisely, to the slope multiplied by -1) passing through the consumption bundle in question, at that point: mathematically, it is the implicit derivative. MRS of Y for X is the amount of Y for which a consumer is willing to exchange for X locally.

a. Demand vacuum
b. Supply and demand
c. Quality bias
d. Marginal rate of substitution

Chapter 3. Factor Endowments and the Commodity Composition of Trade

1. _____s is the social science that studies the production, distribution, and consumption of goods and services. The term _____s comes from the Ancient Greek οἰκονομία from οἶκος (oikos, 'house') + νόμος (nomos, 'custom' or 'law'), hence 'rules of the house(hold)'. Current _____ models developed out of the broader field of political economy in the late 19th century, owing to a desire to use an empirical approach more akin to the physical sciences.
   a. Energy economics
   b. Opportunity cost
   c. Inflation
   d. Economic

2. _____ was a Swedish economist and politician. He was a professor of economics at the Stockholm School of Economics from 1929 to 1965. He was also leader of the People's Party, a social-liberal party which at the time was the largest party in opposition to the governing Social Democratic Party, from 1944 to 1967.
   a. Maximilian Carl Emil Weber
   b. Martin Luther
   c. Nicholas II
   d. Bertil Gotthard Ohlin

3. In production, returns to scale refers to changes in output subsequent to a proportional change in all inputs (where all inputs increase by a constant factor.) If output increases by that same proportional change then there are _____ If output increases by less than that proportional change, there are decreasing returns to scale (DRS.)
   a. Long term
   b. Lexicographic preferences
   c. Consumer sovereignty
   d. Constant returns to scale

4. In economics, _____ are the resources employed to produce goods and services. They facilitate production but do not become part of the product (as with raw materials) or significantly transformed by the production process (as with fuel used to power machinery.) To 19th century economists, the _____ were land (natural resources, gifts from nature), labor (the ability to work), and capital goods (human-made tools and equipment.)
   a. Factors of production
   b. Product Pipeline
   c. Hicks-neutral technical change
   d. Long-run

5. In neoclassical economics and microeconomics, _____ describes the perfect being a market in which there are many small firms, all producing homogeneous goods. In the short term, such markets are productively inefficient as output will not occur where mc is equal to ac, but allocatively efficient, as output under _____ will always occur where mc is equal to mr, and therefore where mc equals ar. However, in the long term, such markets are both allocatively and productively efficient.
   a. Law of supply
   b. General equilibrium
   c. Co-operative economics
   d. Perfect competition

6. In economics, _____ is the total supply of goods and services produced by a national economy during a specific time period. It is the total amount of goods and services in the economy available at all possible price levels.
   a. Aggregate demand
   b. Aggregation problem
   c. Aggregate expenditure
   d. Aggregate supply

7. In microeconomics, _____ is quite simply the conversion of inputs into outputs. It is an economic process that uses resources to create a good or service that is suitable for exchange. This can include manufacturing, storing, shipping, and packaging.
   a. Red Guards
   b. Solved
   c. MET
   d. Production

8. In economics, _____ and economies of scale are related terms that describe what happens as the scale of production increases. They are different terms and should not be used interchangeably.

Chapter 3. Factor Endowments and the Commodity Composition of Trade

_____ refers to a technical property of production that examines changes in output subsequent to a proportional change in all inputs (where all inputs increase by a constant factor.)

a. Necessity good
b. Customer equity
c. Constant returns to scale
d. Returns to scale

9. Capital intensity is the term in economics for the amount of fixed or real capital present in relation to other factors of production, especially labor. At the level of either a production process or the aggregate economy, it may be estimated by the capital/labor ratio, such as from the points along a capital/labor isoquant.

Since the use of tools and machinery makes labor more effective, rising capital intensity (or 'capital deepening') pushes up the productivity of labor, so a society that is more _____ tends to have a higher standard of living over the long run than one with low capital intensity.

a. Capital flight
b. Wealth inequality in the United States
c. Modigliani-Miller theorem
d. Capital intensive

10. In economics a country's _____ is commonly understood as the amount of land, labor, capital, and entrepreneurship that a country possesses and can exploit for manufacturing. Countries with a large endowment of resources tend to be more prosperous than those with a small endowment, all other things being equal. The development of sound institutions to access and equitably distribute these resources, however, is necessary in order for a country to obtain the greatest benefit from its _____.

a. Factor endowment
b. Foreign Affiliate Trade Statistics
c. Price scissors
d. Dutch disease

11. A _____ is an expression that compares quantities relative to each other. The most common examples involve two quantities, but any number of quantities can be compared. _____s are represented mathematically by separating each quantity with a colon, for example the _____ 2:3, which is read as the _____ 'two to three'.

a. Y-intercept
b. 130-30 fund
c. 100-year flood
d. Ratio

12. _____ are the prices that the factors of production of a finished item attract.

There has been some economic debate as to what determines these prices. Classical and Marxist economists argued that the _____ decided the value of a product and so value was intrinsic within the product.

a. Factor prices
b. Marginal product of labor
c. Productivity model
d. Marginal product

13. _____ in economics and business is the result of an exchange and from that trade we assign a numerical monetary value to a good, service or asset. If Alice trades Bob 4 apples for an orange, the _____ of an orange is 4 apples. Inversely, the _____ of an apple is 1/4 oranges.

a. Premium pricing
b. Price war
c. Price book
d. Price

Chapter 3. Factor Endowments and the Commodity Composition of Trade

14. The _____ or gross domestic income (GDI), a basic measure of an economy's economic performance, is the market value of all final goods and services produced within the borders of a nation in a year. _____ can be defined in three ways, all of which are conceptually identical. First, it is equal to the total expenditures for all final goods and services produced within the country in a stipulated period of time (usually a 365-day year.)

  a. Monopolistic competition
  b. Market structure
  c. Countercyclical
  d. Gross domestic product

15. _____ is a misspelled phrase from Latin 'pro capite' phrase meaning per head with pro meaning 'per' or 'for each' and capite meaning 'head.' Both words together equate to the phrase 'for each head.'

It is usually used in the field of statistics to indicate the average per person for any given concern, such as income, crime rate, etc.

It is also used in wills to indicate that each of the named beneficiaries should receive, by devise or bequest, equal shares of the estate. This is in contrast to a per stirpes division, in which each branch of the inheriting family inherits an equal share of the estate.

  a. Per capita
  b. Population statistics
  c. False positive rate
  d. Sargan test

16. The field of _____ looks at the relationship between management and workers, particularly groups of workers represented by a union.

Labor relations is an important factor in analyzing 'varieties of capitalism', such as neocorporatism, social democracy, and neoliberalism

Labor relations can take place on many levels, such as the 'shop-floor', the regional level, and the national level.

  a. ACEA agreement
  b. AD-IA Model
  c. Industrial Relations
  d. ACCRA Cost of Living Index

17. _____ is a program of the United States Department of Labor that provides a variety of reemployment services and benefits to workers who have lost their jobs or suffered a reduction of hours and wages as a result of increased imports or shifts in production outside the United States. The _____ program aims to help program participants obtain new jobs, ensuring they retain employment and earn wages comparable to their prior employment.

_____ was established as part of the Trade Expansion Act in 1962, during the Presidency of John F. Kennedy.

  a. Delancey Street Foundation
  b. Financial Crimes Enforcement Network
  c. New Economic Policy
  d. Trade Adjustment Assistance

18. _____ is the a method of technical and economic research of the systems for purpose to optimize a parity between system's consumer functions or properties and expenses to achieve those functions or properties.

Chapter 3. Factor Endowments and the Commodity Composition of Trade

This methodology for continuous perfection of production, industrial technologies, organizational structures was developed by Juryj Sobolev in 1948 at the 'Perm telephone factory'

- 1948 Juryj Sobolev - the first success in application of a method analysis at the 'Perm telephone factory'.
- 1949 - the first application for the invention as result of use of the new method.

Today in economically developed countries practically each enterprise or the company use methodology of the kind of functional-cost analysis as a practice of the quality management, most full satisfying to principles of standards of series ISO 9000.

- Interest of consumer not in products itself, but the advantage which it will receive from its usage.
- The consumer aspires to reduce his expenses
- Functions needed by consumer can be executed in the various ways, and, hence, with various efficiency and expenses. Among possible alternatives of realization of functions exist such in which the parity of quality and the price is the optimal for the consumer.

The goal of _____ is achievement of the highest consumer satisfaction of production at simultaneous decrease in all kinds of industrial expenses Classical _____ has three English synonyms - Value Engineering, Value Management, Value Analysis.

a. Willingness to pay
b. Staple financing
c. Monopoly wage
d. Function cost analysis

19. _____ refers to the additional value of a commodity over the cost of commodities used to produce it from the previous stage of production. An example is the price of gasoline at the pump over the price of the oil in it. In national accounts used in macroeconomics, it refers to the contribution of the factors of production, i.e., land, labor, and capital goods, to raising the value of a product and corresponds to the incomes received by the owners of these factors.

a. Full employment
b. Solow residual
c. Value added
d. Hodrick-Prescott filter

20. _____ , or goods and services tax (GST) is a consumption tax levied on value added. In contrast to sales tax, _____ is neutral with respect to the number of passages that there are between the producer and the final consumer; where sales tax is levied on total value at each stage, the result is a cascade (downstream taxes levied on upstream taxes.) A _____ is an indirect tax, in that the tax is collected from someone who does not bear the entire cost of the tax.

a. 100-year flood
b. 130-30 fund
c. Value added tax
d. 1921 recession

21. In economics, the _____ or marginal physical product is the extra output produced by one more unit of an input (for instance, the difference in output when a firm's labour is increased from five to six units.) Assuming that no other inputs to production change, the _____ of a given input (X) can be expressed as:

Chapter 3. Factor Endowments and the Commodity Composition of Trade

_____ = ΔY/ΔX = (the change of Y)/(the change of X.)

-
  - ○
    - ■ Pending approval by Thomas Sowell***

In neoclassical economics, this is the mathematical derivative of the production function.... Note that the 'product' (Y) is typically defined ignoring external costs and benefits.

a. Labor problem
c. Productive capacity
b. Marginal product
d. Factor prices

22. To _____ is to impose a financial charge or other levy upon a taxpayer by a state or the functional equivalent of a state.

_____es are also imposed by many subnational entities. _____es consist of direct _____ or indirect _____, and may be paid in money or as its labour equivalent (often but not always unpaid.)

a. 130-30 fund
c. 100-year flood
b. 1921 recession
d. Tax

23. In economics, an _____ is any good or commodity, transported from one country to another country in a legitimate fashion, typically for use in trade. _____ goods or services are provided to foreign consumers by domestic producers. _____ is an important part of international trade.

a. AD-IA Model
c. ACCRA Cost of Living Index
b. ACEA agreement
d. Export

24. In economics, an _____ is any good (e.g. a commodity) or service brought into one country from another country in a legitimate fashion, typically for use in trade. It is a good that is brought in from another country for sale. _____ goods or services are provided to domestic consumers by foreign producers. An _____ in the receiving country is an export to the sending country.

a. Incoterms
c. Economic integration
b. Import quota
d. Import

25. In international economics and international trade, _____ or _____ is the relative prices of a country's export to import. '_____' are sometimes used as a proxy for the relative social welfare of a country, but this heuristic is technically questionable and should be used with extreme caution. An improvement in a nation's _____ is good for that country in the sense that it has to pay less for the products it import.

a. Terms of trade
c. Commercial invoice
b. Kennedy Round
d. Common market

26. The _____ is the apparent contradiction that although water is on the whole more useful, in terms of survival, than diamonds, diamonds command a higher price in the market. The economist Adam Smith is often considered to be the classic presenter of this paradox. Nicolaus Copernicus, John Locke, John Law and others had previously tried to explain the disparity.

Chapter 3. Factor Endowments and the Commodity Composition of Trade

a. St. Petersburg paradox
b. Paradox of value
c. 130-30 fund
d. 100-year flood

27. _____ refers to the stock of skills and knowledge embodied in the ability to perform labor so as to produce economic value. It is the skills and knowledge gained by a worker through education and experience. Many early economic theories refer to it simply as labor, one of three factors of production, and consider it to be a fungible resource -- homogeneous and easily interchangeable. Other conceptions of labor dispense with these assumptions.
   a. Price theory
   b. Law of increasing costs
   c. Human capital
   d. General equilibrium

28. _____ originally was the term for studying production, buying and selling, and their relations with law, custom, and government. _____ originated in moral philosophy. It developed in the 18th century as the study of the economies of states -- polities, hence _____.
   a. Geoeconomics
   b. Productive and unproductive labour
   c. Political Economy
   d. Dirigisme

29. The phrase _____, according to the Organization for Economic Co-operation and Development, refers to 'creative work undertaken on a systematic basis in order to increase the stock of knowledge, including knowledge of man, culture and society, and the use of this stock of knowledge to devise new applications [sic]'

New product design and development is more than often a crucial factor in the survival of a company. In an industry that is fast changing, firms must continually revise their design and range of products. This is necessary due to continuous technology change and development as well as other competitors and the changing preference of customers.

   a. Research and Development
   b. 130-30 fund
   c. 100-year flood
   d. 1921 recession

30. _____ is money accepted for exchange of goods in an economy. The prevalence of one money over another arises, usually, when a government designates through decrees that the government shall accept only particular notes and coins in payment for taxes. Typically, money of _____ consists of stamped coins and minted paper bills.
   a. Security thread
   b. Totnes pound
   c. Local currency
   d. Currency

31. A _____ is a monetary authority which is required to maintain a fixed exchange rate with a foreign currency. This policy objective requires the conventional objectives of a central bank to be subordinated to the exchange rate target.

20 Chapter 3. Factor Endowments and the Commodity Composition of Trade

The main qualities of an orthodox _____ are:

- A _____'s foreign currency reserves must be sufficient to ensure that all holders of its notes and coins (and all banks creditor of a Reserve Account at the _____) can convert them into the reserve currency (usually 110-115% of the monetary base M0.)
- A _____ maintains absolute, unlimited convertibility between its notes and coins and the currency against which they are pegged (the anchor currency), at a fixed rate of exchange, with no restrictions on current-account or capital-account transactions.
- A _____ only earns profit from interests on foreign reserves (less the expense of note-issuing), and does not engage in forward-exchange transactions. These foreign reserves exist (1) because local notes have been issued in exchange, or (2) because commercial banks must by regulation deposit a minimum reserve at the _____. (1) generates a seignorage revenue. (2) is the revenue on minimum reserves (revenue of investment activities less cost of minimum reserves remuneration)
- A _____ has no discretionary powers to effect monetary policy and does not lend to the government. Governments cannot print money, and can only tax or borrow to meet their spending commitments.
- A _____ does not act as a lender of last resort to commercial banks, and does not regulate reserve requirements.
- A _____ does not attempt to manipulate interest rates by establishing a discount rate like a central bank. The peg with the foreign currency tends to keep interest rates and inflation very closely aligned to those in the country against whose currency the peg is fixed.

The _____ in question will no longer issue fiat money but instead will only issue one unit of local currency for each unit (or decided amount) of foreign currency it has in its vault (often a hard currency such as the U.S. dollar or the euro.) The surplus on the balance of payments of that country is reflected by higher deposits local banks hold at the central bank as well as (initially) higher deposits of the (net) exporting firms at their local banks.

a. Petrodollar
b. Currency competition
c. Reserve currency
d. Currency board

32. Economics:

- _____, the desire to own something and the ability to pay for it
- _____ curve, a graphic representation of a _____ schedule
- _____ deposit, the money in checking accounts
- _____ pull theory, the theory that inflation occurs when _____ for goods and services exceeds existing supplies
- _____ schedule, a table that lists the quantity of a good a person will buy it each different price
- _____ side economics, the school of economics at believes government spending and tax cuts open economy by raising _____

a. Variability
b. McKesson ' Robbins scandal
c. Production
d. Demand

33. _____ is a branch of economics with three main subdisciplines international trade, monetary economics and international finance.

- International trade studies goods-and-services flows across international boundaries from supply-and-demand factors, economic integration, and policy variables such as tariff rates and trade quotas.
- International finance studies the flow of capital across international financial markets, and the effects of these movements on exchange rates.
- International monetary economics and macroeconomics studies money and macro flows across countries.

- Stanley W. Black (2008.) 'international monetary institutions,' The New Palgrave Dictionary of Economics. 2nd Edition.

a. International Economics
b. Index number
c. ACCRA Cost of Living Index
d. Economic depreciation

Chapter 4. Intraindustry Trade

1. _____s is the social science that studies the production, distribution, and consumption of goods and services. The term _____s comes from the Ancient Greek οἰκονομία from οἶκος (oikos, 'house') + νόμος (nomos, 'custom' or 'law'), hence 'rules of the house(hold)'. Current _____ models developed out of the broader field of political economy in the late 19th century, owing to a desire to use an empirical approach more akin to the physical sciences.
   a. Energy economics
   b. Opportunity cost
   c. Inflation
   d. Economic

2. _____ in its classic form is defined as a company from one country making a physical investment into building a factory in another country. It is the establishment of an enterprise by a foreigner. Its definition can be extended to include investments made to acquire lasting interest in enterprises operating outside of the economy of the investor.
   a. Financial Stability Forum
   b. Non-governmental organization
   c. Federal Deposit Insurance Corporation
   d. Foreign direct investment

3. The _____ is an international organization that oversees the global financial system by following the macroeconomic policies of its member countries, in particular those with an impact on exchange rates and the balance of payments. It is an organization formed to stabilize international exchange rates and facilitate development. It also offers financial and technical assistance to its members, making it an international lender of last resort.
   a. ACCRA Cost of Living Index
   b. ACEA agreement
   c. Office of Thrift Supervision
   d. International Monetary Fund

4. A _____ is an object whose consumption increases the utility of the consumer, for which the quantity demanded exceeds the quantity supplied at zero price. _____s are usually modeled as having diminishing marginal utility. The first individual purchase has high utility; the second has less.
   a. Merit good
   b. Pie method
   c. Composite good
   d. Good

5. The _____ is a treaty of the World Trade Organization (WTO) that entered into force in January 1995 as a result of the Uruguay Round negotiations. The treaty was created to extend the multilateral trading system to service sector, in the same way the General Agreement on Tariffs and Trade (GATT) provides such a system for merchandise trade.

All members of the WTO are signatories to the GATS.

   a. General Agreement on Tariffs and Trade
   b. Dutch-Scandinavian Economic Pact
   c. GATT
   d. General Agreement on Trade in Services

6. In economic theory, _____ is the competitive situation in any market where the conditions necessary for perfect competition are not satisfied. It is a market structure that does not meet the conditions of perfect competition.

Forms of _____ include:

- Monopoly, in which there is only one seller of a good.
- Oligopoly, in which there is a small number of sellers.
- Monopolistic competition, in which there are many sellers producing highly differentiated goods.
- Monopsony, in which there is only one buyer of a good.
- Oligopsony, in which there is a small number of buyers.

Chapter 4. Intraindustry Trade

There may also be _____ in markets due to buyers or sellers lacking information about prices and the goods being traded.

There may also be _____ due to a time lag in a market.

   a. AD-IA Model
   b. ACCRA Cost of Living Index
   c. ACEA agreement
   d. Imperfect competition

7. _____ is a branch of economics with three main subdisciplines international trade, monetary economics and international finance.

- International trade studies goods-and-services flows across international boundaries from supply-and-demand factors, economic integration, and policy variables such as tariff rates and trade quotas.
- International finance studies the flow of capital across international financial markets, and the effects of these movements on exchange rates.
- International monetary economics and macroeconomics studies money and macro flows across countries.
- Stanley W. Black (2008.) 'international monetary institutions,' The New Palgrave Dictionary of Economics. 2nd Edition.

   a. Economic depreciation
   b. ACCRA Cost of Living Index
   c. Index number
   d. International Economics

8. _____ is a common market structure where many competing producers sell products that are differentiated from one another (ie. the products are substitutes, but are not exactly alike.) Many markets are monopolistically competitive, common examples include the markets for restaurants, cereal, clothing, shoes and service industries in large cities.

   a. Financial crisis
   b. Mathematical economics
   c. Perfect competition
   d. Monopolistic competition

9. In neoclassical economics and microeconomics, _____ describes the perfect being a market in which there are many small firms, all producing homogeneous goods. In the short term, such markets are productively inefficient as output will not occur where mc is equal to ac, but allocatively efficient, as output under _____ will always occur where mc is equal to mr, and therefore where mc equals ar. However, in the long term, such markets are both allocatively and productively efficient.

   a. Co-operative economics
   b. General equilibrium
   c. Perfect competition
   d. Law of supply

10. _____, in microeconomics, are the cost advantages that a business obtains due to expansion. They are factors that cause a producere;s average cost per unit to fall as scale is increased. _____ is a long run concept and refers to reductions in unit cost as the size of a facility, or scale, increases.

   a. Economic production quantity
   b. Economies of scale
   c. Isoquant
   d. Underinvestment employment relationship

Chapter 4. Intraindustry Trade

11. In economics, a _____ exists when a specific individual or enterprise has sufficient control over a particular product or service to determine significantly the terms on which other individuals shall have access to it. Monopolies are thus characterized by a lack of economic competition for the good or service that they provide and a lack of viable substitute goods. The verb 'monopolize' refers to the process by which a firm gains persistently greater market share than what is expected under perfect competition.

   a. 1921 recession
   b. 100-year flood
   c. Monopoly
   d. 130-30 fund

12. An _____ is a market form in which a market or industry is dominated by a small number of sellers (oligopolists.) Because there are few participants in this type of market, each oligopolist is aware of the actions of the others. The decisions of one firm influence, and are influenced by, the decisions of other firms.

   a. ACEA agreement
   b. ACCRA Cost of Living Index
   c. Oligopsony
   d. Oligopoly

13. An example of _____ is when a company is cut in size but the remaining firms still hold the same amount of final output. Therefore the company has become more efficient in production and has experienced _____ .the internal part of the business expands enabling the business to make higher profits.

   Six main types of _____ can be defined.

   a. ACCRA Cost of Living Index
   b. ACEA agreement
   c. AD-IA Model
   d. Internal Economies of scale

14. _____ originally was the term for studying production, buying and selling, and their relations with law, custom, and government. _____ originated in moral philosophy. It developed in the 18th century as the study of the economies of states -- polities, hence _____ .

   a. Geoeconomics
   b. Productive and unproductive labour
   c. Dirigisme
   d. Political Economy

15. Economics:

   - _____ ,the desire to own something and the ability to pay for it
   - _____ curve,a graphic representation of a _____ schedule
   - _____ deposit, the money in checking accounts
   - _____ pull theory,the theory that inflation occurs when _____ for goods and services exceeds existing supplies
   - _____ schedule,a table that lists the quantity of a good a person will buy it each different price
   - _____ side economics,the school of economics at believes government spending and tax cuts open economy by raising _____

   a. Variability
   b. Demand
   c. McKesson ' Robbins scandal
   d. Production

16. _____ is exchange of capital, goods, and services across international borders or territories. In most countries, it represents a significant share of gross domestic product (GDP.) While _____ has been present throughout much of history, its economic, social, and political importance has been on the rise in recent centuries.

a. International Trade
b. Incoterms
c. Import license
d. Intra-industry trade

Chapter 5. International Factor Movements

1. _____ to the arrival of new individuals into a habitat or population. It is a biological concept and is important in population ecology, differentiated from emigration and migration.

   _____ is a modern phenomenon.

   a. ACEA agreement
   c. AD-IA Model
   b. ACCRA Cost of Living Index
   d. Immigration

2. _____ or human capital flight is a large emigration of individuals with technical skills or knowledge, normally due to conflict, lack of opportunity, political instability, or health risks. _____ is usually regarded as an economic cost, since emigrants usually take with them the fraction of value of their training sponsored by the government. It is a parallel of capital flight which refers to the same movement of financial capital.

   a. 1921 recession
   c. 100-year flood
   b. 130-30 fund
   d. Brain drain

3. _____s is the social science that studies the production, distribution, and consumption of goods and services. The term _____s comes from the Ancient Greek oá¼°κονομῖα from oá¼¶κος (oikos, 'house') + vĺŒμος (nomos, 'custom' or 'law'), hence 'rules of the house(hold)'. Current _____ models developed out of the broader field of political economy in the late 19th century, owing to a desire to use an empirical approach more akin to the physical sciences.

   a. Energy economics
   c. Opportunity cost
   b. Inflation
   d. Economic

4. _____ is exchange of capital, goods, and services across international borders or territories. In most countries, it represents a significant share of gross domestic product (GDP.) While _____ has been present throughout much of history , its economic, social, and political importance has been on the rise in recent centuries.

   a. Incoterms
   c. International trade
   b. Intra-industry trade
   d. Import license

5. _____ in its classic form is defined as a company from one country making a physical investment into building a factory in another country. It is the establishment of an enterprise by a foreigner. Its definition can be extended to include investments made to acquire lasting interest in enterprises operating outside of the economy of the investor.

   a. Foreign direct investment
   c. Financial Stability Forum
   b. Non-governmental organization
   d. Federal Deposit Insurance Corporation

6. _____ can be generally defined as the course of action or inaction taken by governmental entities with regard to a particular issue or set of issues. Other scholars define it as a system of 'courses of action, regulatory measures, laws, and funding priorities concerning a given topic promulgated by a governmental entity or its representatives.' _____ is commonly embodied 'in constitutions, legislative acts, and judicial decisions.'

In the United States, this concept refers not only to the end result of policies, but more broadly to the decision-making and analysis of governmental decisions. _____ is also considered an academic discipline, as it is studied by professors and students at _____ schools of major universities throughout the country.

   a. 130-30 fund
   c. 100-year flood
   b. 1921 recession
   d. Public policy

Chapter 5. International Factor Movements

7. Economics:

   - _____, the desire to own something and the ability to pay for it
   - _____ curve, a graphic representation of a _____ schedule
   - _____ deposit, the money in checking accounts
   - _____ pull theory, the theory that inflation occurs when _____ for goods and services exceeds existing supplies
   - _____ schedule, a table that lists the quantity of a good a person will buy it each different price
   - _____ side economics, the school of economics at believes government spending and tax cuts open economy by raising _____

   a. Variability
   b. McKesson ' Robbins scandal
   c. Production
   d. Demand

8. In economics, an _____ is any good or commodity, transported from one country to another country in a legitimate fashion, typically for use in trade. _____ goods or services are provided to foreign consumers by domestic producers. _____ is an important part of international trade.

   a. ACCRA Cost of Living Index
   b. AD-IA Model
   c. Export
   d. ACEA agreement

9. In economics, an _____ is any good (e.g. a commodity) or service brought into one country from another country in a legitimate fashion, typically for use in trade. It is a good that is brought in from another country for sale. _____ goods or services are provided to domestic consumers by foreign producers. An _____ in the receiving country is an export to the sending country.

   a. Import quota
   b. Import
   c. Economic integration
   d. Incoterms

10. _____ refers to the dynamic process whereby the living cultures of the world are changing and adapting to external or internal forces. This process is occurring within Western culture as well as non-Western and indigenous cultures and cultures of the world

    a. 1921 recession
    b. 130-30 fund
    c. 100-year flood
    d. Transformation of culture

11. _____ is the development of economic wealth of countries or regions for the well-being of their inhabitants. It is the process by which a nation improves the economic, political, and social well being of its people. From a policy perspective, _____ can be defined as efforts that seek to improve the economic well-being and quality of life for a community by creating and/or retaining jobs and supporting or growing incomes and the tax base.

    a. Economic methodology
    b. Experimental economics
    c. Inflation
    d. Economic Development

12. A _____ is an expression that compares quantities relative to each other. The most common examples involve two quantities, but any number of quantities can be compared. _____s are represented mathematically by separating each quantity with a colon, for example the _____ 2:3, which is read as the _____ 'two to three'.

a. 130-30 fund
b. Y-intercept
c. Ratio
d. 100-year flood

13. A _____ or transnational corporation is a corporation or enterprise that manages production or delivers services in more than one country. It can also be referred to as an international corporation.

The first modern MNC is generally thought to be the Dutch East India Company, established in 1602.

a. Multinational corporation
b. Rakon
c. Foreign direct investment
d. Luxembourg Income Study

14. _____ is subcontracting a process, such as product design or manufacturing, to a third-party company. The decision to outsource is often made in the interest of lowering cost or making better use of time and energy costs, redirecting or conserving energy directed at the competencies of a particular business, or to make more efficient use of land, labor, capital, (information) technology and resources. _____ became part of the business lexicon during the 1980s.

a. Additional Funds Needed
b. Electronic business
c. Averch-Johnson effect
d. Outsourcing

15. The _____ consists of a number of economic theories which describe the nature of the firm, company including its existence, its behaviour, and its relationship with the market.

In simplified terms, the _____ aims to answer these questions:

1. Existence - why do firms emerge, why are not all transactions in the economy mediated over the market?
2. Boundaries - why the boundary between firms and the market is located exactly there? Which transactions are performed internally and which are negotiated on the market?
3. Organization - why are firms structured in such specific way? What is the interplay of formal and informal relationships?

Despite looking simple, these questions are not answered by the established economic theory, which usually views firms as given, and treats them as black boxes without any internal structure.

The First World War period saw a change of emphasis in economic theory away from industry-level analysis which mainly included analysing markets to analysis at the level of the firm, as it became increasingly clear that perfect competition was no longer an adequate model of how firms behaved. Economic theory till then had focussed on trying to understand markets alone and there had been little study on understanding why firms or organisations exist.

a. Khazzoom-Brookes postulate
b. Technology gap
c. Policy Ineffectiveness Proposition
d. Theory of the firm

16. The _____ or gross domestic income (GDI), a basic measure of an economy's economic performance, is the market value of all final goods and services produced within the borders of a nation in a year. _____ can be defined in three ways, all of which are conceptually identical. First, it is equal to the total expenditures for all final goods and services produced within the country in a stipulated period of time (usually a 365-day year.)

Chapter 5. International Factor Movements

a. Gross domestic product
b. Countercyclical
c. Market structure
d. Monopolistic competition

17. A _____ is an entity formed between two or more parties to undertake economic activity together. The parties agree to create a new entity by both contributing equity, and they then share in the revenues, expenses, and control of the enterprise. The venture can be for one specific project only, or a continuing business relationship such as the Fuji Xerox _____.
   a. Property right
   b. Business valuation
   c. Nexus of contracts
   d. Joint venture

18. In business and accounting, _____ are everything of value that is owned by a person or company. It is a claim on the property your income of a borrower. The balance sheet of a firm records the monetary value of the _____ owned by the firm.
   a. Amortization schedule
   b. ACCRA Cost of Living Index
   c. Assets
   d. ACEA agreement

19. An _____ is a person who has possession of an enterprise and assumes significant accountability for the inherent risks and the outcome. It is an ambitious leader who combines land, labor, and capital to create and market new goods or services. The term is a loanword from French and was first defined by the Irish economist Richard Cantillon.
   a. Expansionary policies
   b. ACEA agreement
   c. Entrepreneur
   d. ACCRA Cost of Living Index

20. A _____ is one scenario provided for evaluation by respondents in a Choice Experiment. Responses are collected and used to create a Choice Model. Respondents are usually provided with a series of differing _____s for evaluation.
   a. 1921 recession
   b. 130-30 fund
   c. Choice Set
   d. 100-year flood

21. _____ refers to the pricing of contributions (assets, tangible and intangible, services, and funds) transferred within an organization. For example, goods from the production division may be sold to the marketing division, or goods from a parent company may be sold to a foreign subsidiary. Since the prices are set within an organization (i.e. controlled), the typical market mechanisms that establish prices for such transactions between third parties may not apply.
   a. Rational pricing
   b. Two-part tariff
   c. Transfer pricing
   d. San Francisco congestion pricing

22. _____ is one of the four Ps of the marketing mix. The other three aspects are product, promotion, and place. It is also a key variable in microeconomic price allocation theory.
   a. Premium pricing
   b. Point of total assumption
   c. Guaranteed Maximum Price
   d. Pricing

Chapter 6. Tariffs

1. In microeconomics, _____ is quite simply the conversion of inputs into outputs. It is an economic process that uses resources to create a good or service that is suitable for exchange. This can include manufacturing, storing, shipping, and packaging.
   - a. MET
   - b. Production
   - c. Solved
   - d. Red Guards

2. A _____ is a duty imposed on goods when they are moved across a political boundary. They are usually associated with protectionism, the economic policy of restraining trade between nations. For political reasons, _____s are usually imposed on imported goods, although they may also be imposed on exported goods.
   - a. Tariff
   - b. 100-year flood
   - c. 1921 recession
   - d. 130-30 fund

3. _____, in law and economics, is a form of risk management primarily used to hedge against the risk of a contingent loss. _____ is defined as the equitable transfer of the risk of a loss, from one entity to another, in exchange for a premium, and can be thought of as a guaranteed small loss to prevent a large, possibly devastating loss. An insurer is a company selling the _____; an insured or policyholder is the person or entity buying the _____.
   - a. ACCRA Cost of Living Index
   - b. AD-IA Model
   - c. ACEA agreement
   - d. Insurance

4. _____ is a broad label that refers to any individuals or households that use goods and services generated within the economy. The concept of a _____ is used in different contexts, so that the usage and significance of the term may vary.
   Typically when business people and economists talk of _____s they are talking about person as _____, an aggregated commodity item with little individuality other than that expressed in the buy/not-buy decision.
   - a. 1921 recession
   - b. 100-year flood
   - c. 130-30 fund
   - d. Consumer

5. The term surplus is used in economics for several related quantities. The _____ is the amount that consumers benefit by being able to purchase a product for a price that is less than they would be willing to pay. The producer surplus is the amount that producers benefit by selling at a market price mechanism that is higher than they would be willing to sell for.
   - a. Necessity good
   - b. Marginal rate of technical substitution
   - c. Microeconomic reform
   - d. Consumer surplus

6. The term surplus is used in economics for several related quantities. The consumer surplus is the amount that consumers benefit by being able to purchase a product for a price that is less than they would be willing to pay. The _____ is the amount that producers benefit by selling at a market price mechanism that is higher than they would be willing to sell for.
   - a. Schedule delay
   - b. Producer surplus
   - c. Long term
   - d. Returns to scale

7. _____ is a type of trade policy that allows traders to act and transact without interference from government. Thus, the policy permits trading partners mutual gains from trade, with goods and services produced according to the theory of comparative advantage.

Chapter 6. Tariffs

Under a _____ policy, prices are a reflection of true supply and demand, and are the sole determinant of resource allocation.

a. Free trade
c. 1921 recession
b. 100-year flood
d. 130-30 fund

8. _____s is the social science that studies the production, distribution, and consumption of goods and services. The term _____s comes from the Ancient Greek οἰκονομία from οἶκος (oikos, 'house') + νόμος (nomos, 'custom' or 'law'), hence 'rules of the house(hold)'. Current _____ models developed out of the broader field of political economy in the late 19th century, owing to a desire to use an empirical approach more akin to the physical sciences.

a. Energy economics
c. Inflation
b. Opportunity cost
d. Economic

9. In economics, the _____ is a measure of the total effect of the entire tariff structure on the value added per unit of output in each industry, when both intermediate and final goods are imported. This statistic is used by economists to measure the real amount of protection afforded to a particular industry by import duties, tariffs or other trade restrictions.

Consider a simple case, there is a tradable good (shoes) that uses one tradable input to produce (leather.)

a. IATT
c. Effective rate of protection
b. Export function
d. Aras Free Zone

10. The _____ or gross domestic income (GDI), a basic measure of an economy's economic performance, is the market value of all final goods and services produced within the borders of a nation in a year. _____ can be defined in three ways, all of which are conceptually identical. First, it is equal to the total expenditures for all final goods and services produced within the country in a stipulated period of time (usually a 365-day year.)

a. Countercyclical
c. Market structure
b. Gross domestic product
d. Monopolistic competition

Chapter 7. Nontariff Distortions to Trade

1. In statistics the _____ of an event i is the number n_i of times the event occurred in the experiment or the study. These frequencies are often graphically represented in histograms.

   We speak of absolute frequencies, when the counts n_i themselves are given and of (relative) frequencies, when those are normalized by the total number of events:

   $$f_i = \frac{n_i}{N} = \frac{n_i}{\sum_i n_i}.$$

   Taking the f_i for all i and tabulating or plotting them leads to a _____ distribution.

   a. 1921 recession
   b. 130-30 fund
   c. 100-year flood
   d. Frequency

2. In economics, an _____ is any good or commodity, transported from one country to another country in a legitimate fashion, typically for use in trade. _____ goods or services are provided to foreign consumers by domestic producers. _____ is an important part of international trade.

   a. AD-IA Model
   b. ACCRA Cost of Living Index
   c. Export
   d. ACEA agreement

3. _____ is a broad label that refers to any individuals or households that use goods and services generated within the economy. The concept of a _____ is used in different contexts, so that the usage and significance of the term may vary.

   Typically when business people and economists talk of _____s they are talking about person as _____, an aggregated commodity item with little individuality other than that expressed in the buy/not-buy decision.

   a. 1921 recession
   b. 130-30 fund
   c. 100-year flood
   d. Consumer

4. The term surplus is used in economics for several related quantities. The _____ is the amount that consumers benefit by being able to purchase a product for a price that is less than they would be willing to pay. The producer surplus is the amount that producers benefit by selling at a market price mechanism that is higher than they would be willing to sell for.

   a. Marginal rate of technical substitution
   b. Consumer surplus
   c. Microeconomic reform
   d. Necessity good

5. The term surplus is used in economics for several related quantities. The consumer surplus is the amount that consumers benefit by being able to purchase a product for a price that is less than they would be willing to pay. The _____ is the amount that producers benefit by selling at a market price mechanism that is higher than they would be willing to sell for.

   a. Returns to scale
   b. Long term
   c. Schedule delay
   d. Producer surplus

Chapter 7. Nontariff Distortions to Trade

6. _____s is the social science that studies the production, distribution, and consumption of goods and services. The term _____s comes from the Ancient Greek οá¼°κονομῖα from οá¼¶κος (oikos, 'house') + vÍŒμος (nomos, 'custom' or 'law'), hence 'rules of the house(hold)'. Current _____ models developed out of the broader field of political economy in the late 19th century, owing to a desire to use an empirical approach more akin to the physical sciences.
   a. Opportunity cost
   b. Energy economics
   c. Inflation
   d. Economic

7. A _____ is a duty imposed on goods when they are moved across a political boundary. They are usually associated with protectionism, the economic policy of restraining trade between nations. For political reasons, _____s are usually imposed on imported goods, although they may also be imposed on exported goods.
   a. Tariff
   b. 130-30 fund
   c. 1921 recession
   d. 100-year flood

8. Economics:

   - _____,the desire to own something and the ability to pay for it
   - _____ curve,a graphic representation of a _____ schedule
   - _____ deposit, the money in checking accounts
   - _____ pull theory,the theory that inflation occurs when _____ for goods and services exceeds existing supplies
   - _____ schedule,a table that lists the quantity of a good a person will buy it each different price
   - _____ side economics,the school of economics at believes government spending and tax cuts open economy by raising _____

   a. Variability
   b. McKesson ' Robbins scandal
   c. Demand
   d. Production

9. _____ was a survey conducted by the U.S. Department of Justice to gauge the prevalence of alcohol and illegal drug use among prior arrestees. It was a reformulation of the prior Drug Use Forecasting (DUF) program, focused on five drugs in particular: cocaine, marijuana, methamphetamine, opiates, and PCP.

Participants were randomly selected from arrest records in major metropolitan areas; because no personally identifying information is taken from each record chosen, the resulting data can be correlated to arrest rates, but not to the total population of persons charged.

   a. AD-IA Model
   b. ACCRA Cost of Living Index
   c. ACEA agreement
   d. Arrestee Drug Abuse Monitoring

10. _____ was a Scottish moral philosopher and a pioneer of political economy. One of the key figures of the Scottish Enlightenment, Smith is the author of The Theory of Moral Sentiments and An Inquiry into the Nature and Causes of the Wealth of Nations. The latter, usually abbreviated as The Wealth of Nations, is considered his magnum opus and the first modern work of economics.
    a. Alan Greenspan
    b. Adolf Hitler
    c. Adolph Fischer
    d. Adam Smith

11. In economics, _____ refers to the ability of a party to produce a good or service using fewer real resources than another entity producing the same good or service..A party has an _____ when using the same input as another party, it can produce a greater output. Since _____ is determined by a simple comparison of labor productivities, it is possible for a a party to have no _____ in anything. It can be contrasted with the concept of comparative advantage which refers to the ability to produce a particular good at a lower opportunity cost.
   a. International economics
   b. Index number
   c. ACCRA Cost of Living Index
   d. Absolute advantage

12. _____ is the acquisition of goods and/or services at the best possible total cost of ownership, in the right quantity and quality, at the right time, in the right place and from the right source for the direct benefit or use of corporations or individuals, generally via a contract. Simple _____ may involve nothing more than repeat purchasing. Complex _____ could involve finding long term partners - or even 'co-destiny' suppliers that might fundamentally commit one organization to another.
   a. Sole proprietorship
   b. Golden umbrella
   c. Pre-emerging markets
   d. Procurement

13. _____ or human capital flight is a large emigration of individuals with technical skills or knowledge, normally due to conflict, lack of opportunity, political instability, or health risks. _____ is usually regarded as an economic cost, since emigrants usually take with them the fraction of value of their training sponsored by the government. It is a parallel of capital flight which refers to the same movement of financial capital.
   a. 1921 recession
   b. 130-30 fund
   c. 100-year flood
   d. Brain drain

14. The _____ is an international organization that oversees the global financial system by following the macroeconomic policies of its member countries, in particular those with an impact on exchange rates and the balance of payments. It is an organization formed to stabilize international exchange rates and facilitate development. It also offers financial and technical assistance to its members, making it an international lender of last resort.
   a. International Monetary Fund
   b. ACCRA Cost of Living Index
   c. ACEA agreement
   d. Office of Thrift Supervision

15. _____ is the graphical representation of Simon Kuznets's theory ('Kuznets hypothesis') that economic inequality increases over time while a country is developing, then after a critical average income is attained, begins to decrease.

One theory as to why this happens states that in early stages of development, when investment in physical capital is the main mechanism of economic growth, inequality encourages growth by allocating resources towards those who save and invest the most. Whereas in mature economies human capital accrual, or an estimate of cost that has been incurred but not yet paid, takes the place of physical capital accrual as the main source of growth, and inequality slows growth by lowering education standards because poor people lack finance for their education in imperfect credit markets.

   a. Demand curve
   b. Cost curve
   c. Wage curve
   d. Kuznets curve

16. A _____ is an object whose consumption increases the utility of the consumer, for which the quantity demanded exceeds the quantity supplied at zero price. _____s are usually modeled as having diminishing marginal utility. The first individual purchase has high utility; the second has less.

a. Good
c. Composite good
b. Merit good
d. Pie method

Chapter 8. International Trade Policy

1. _____s is the social science that studies the production, distribution, and consumption of goods and services. The term _____s comes from the Ancient Greek οἰκονομῖα from οἴκος (oikos, 'house') + νόμος (nomos, 'custom' or 'law'), hence 'rules of the house(hold)'. Current _____ models developed out of the broader field of political economy in the late 19th century, owing to a desire to use an empirical approach more akin to the physical sciences.

    a. Energy economics
    b. Economic
    c. Inflation
    d. Opportunity cost

2. _____ is an approach to legal theory that applies methods of economics to law. It includes the use of economic concepts to explain the effects of laws, to assess which legal rules are economically efficient, and to predict which legal rules will be promulgated.

    As used by lawyers and legal scholars, the phrase '_____' refers to the application of the methods of economics to legal problems.

    a. Law and Economics
    b. Public economics
    c. Georgism
    d. Monopolistic competition

3. _____ in economic theory is the use of modern economic tools to study problems that are traditionally in the province of political science.

    In particular, it studies the behavior of politicians and government officials as mostly self-interested agents and their interactions in the social system either as such or under alternative constitutional rules. These can be represented a number of ways, including standard constrained utility maximization, game theory, or decision theory.

    a. Rational ignorance
    b. Paradox of voting
    c. Public interest theory
    d. Public choice

4. _____ is a fee paid on borrowed assets. It is the price paid for the use of borrowed money , or, money earned by deposited funds . Assets that are sometimes lent with _____ include money, shares, consumer goods through hire purchase, major assets such as aircraft, and even entire factories in finance lease arrangements.

    a. Insolvency
    b. Internal debt
    c. Asset protection
    d. Interest

5. Economic _____ is defined as an excess distribution to any factor in a production process above that which is required to induce the factor into the process or any excess above that which is necessary to keep the factor in its current use..

    Classical Factor _____ is primarily concerned with the fee paid for the use of fixed (e.g. natural) resources. The classical definition is expressed as any excess payment above that required to induce or provide for production.

    a. Rent
    b. 130-30 fund
    c. 100-year flood
    d. 1921 recession

6. In economics, _____ occurs when an individual, organization or firm seeks to make money through economic rent.

Chapter 8. International Trade Policy

_____ generally implies the extraction of uncompensated value from others without making any contribution to productivity, such as by gaining control of land and other pre-existing natural resources, or by imposing burdensome regulations or other government decisions that may affect consumers or businesses. While there may be few people in modern industrialized countries who do not gain something, directly or indirectly, through some form or another of _____, Rent seeking in the aggregate imposes substantial losses on society.

a. 130-30 fund
b. 100-year flood
c. Good governance
d. Rent seeking

7. A _____ is a duty imposed on goods when they are moved across a political boundary. They are usually associated with protectionism, the economic policy of restraining trade between nations. For political reasons, _____s are usually imposed on imported goods, although they may also be imposed on exported goods.

a. 1921 recession
b. 130-30 fund
c. 100-year flood
d. Tariff

8. The _____ is a trilateral trade bloc in North America created by the governments of the United States, Canada, and Mexico. The agreement creating the trade bloc came into force on January 1, 1994. It superseded the Canada-United States Free Trade Agreement between the U.S. and Canada.

a. Federal Reserve Bank Notes
b. Demand-side technologies
c. Case-Shiller Home Price Indices
d. North American Free Trade Agreement

9. In microeconomics, _____ is quite simply the conversion of inputs into outputs. It is an economic process that uses resources to create a good or service that is suitable for exchange. This can include manufacturing, storing, shipping, and packaging.

a. Solved
b. Production
c. Red Guards
d. MET

10. _____ was the first United States Secretary of the Treasury, a Founding Father, economist, and political philosopher. He led calls for the Philadelphia Convention, was one of America's first Constitutional lawyers, and cowrote the Federalist Papers, a primary source for Constitutional interpretation.

Born on the British West Indian island of Nevis, Hamilton was educated in the Thirteen Colonies.

a. Adam Smith
b. American exceptionalism
c. Economic impact of immigration
d. Alexander Hamilton

11. The _____ was an act signed into law on June 17, 1930, that raised U.S. tariffs on over 20,000 imported goods to record levels. In the United States 1,028 economists signed a petition against this legislation, and after it was passed, many countries retaliated with their own increased tariffs on U.S. goods, and American exports and imports were reduced by more than half.

Although rated capacity had increased tremendously, actual output, income, and expenditure had not.

Chapter 8. International Trade Policy

a. Patent Law Treaty
b. Judgment summons
c. Loss of use
d. Smoot-Hawley Tariff Act

12. The _____ provided for the negotiation of tariff agreements between the United States and separate nations, particularly Latin American countries. It resulted in a reduction of duties.

President Franklin D. Roosevelt was authorized by the Act for a fixed period of time to negotiate on bilateral basis with other countries and then implement reductions in tariffs in exchange for compensating tariff reductions by the partner trading country. Roosevelt was also instructed to maximize market access abroad without jeopardizing domestic industry, and reduce tariffs only as necessary to promote exports in accord with the 'needs of various branches of American production.' A most favored nation clause was also included.

a. Reciprocal Trade Agreements Act
b. Patent Law Treaty
c. Long service leave
d. Kaldor-Hicks efficiency

13. The _____ was the outcome of the failure of negotiating governments to create the International Trade Organization (ITO.) GATT was formed in 1947 and lasted until 1994, when it was replaced by the World Trade Organization. The Bretton Woods Conference had introduced the idea for an organization to regulate trade as part of a larger plan for economic recovery after World War II.

a. GATT
b. General Agreement on Trade in Services
c. General Agreement on Tariffs and Trade
d. Dutch-Scandinavian Economic Pact

14. _____ are duties imposed under WTO Rules to neutralize the negative effects of other duties. They are imposed when a foreign country subsidizes its exports, hurting domestic producers in the importing country

a. Market access
b. Kennedy Round
c. Certificate of origin
d. Countervailing duties

15. _____ is exchange of capital, goods, and services across international borders or territories. In most countries, it represents a significant share of gross domestic product (GDP.) While _____ has been present throughout much of history, its economic, social, and political importance has been on the rise in recent centuries.

a. International Trade
b. Incoterms
c. Intra-industry trade
d. Import license

16. The _____ was the sixth session of General Agreement on Tariffs and Trade (GATT) trade negotiations held in 1964-1967 in Geneva, Switzerland. Congressional passage of the US Trade Expansion Act in 1962 authorized the White House to conduct mutual tariff negotiations ultimately leading to the _____. The _____ had four major goals: to slash tariffs by half with a minimum of exceptions, to break down farm trade restrictions, to strip away nontariff regulations, and to aid developing nations.

a. Jamaican Free Zones
b. Special Drawing Rights
c. Heckscher-Ohlin model
d. Kennedy Round

17. The _____ commenced in September 1986 and continued until April 1994. The round, based on the General Agreement on Tariffs and Trade (GATT) ministerial meeting in Geneva (1982), was launched in Punta del Este in Uruguay (hence the name), followed by negotiations in Montreal, Geneva, Brussels, Washington, D.C., and Tokyo, with the 20 agreements finally being signed in Marrakech - the Marrakesh Agreement. The Round transformed the GATT into the World Trade Organization.

a. AD-IA Model
b. ACEA agreement
c. ACCRA Cost of Living Index
d. Uruguay Round

18. The _____ is an important selective, mainly private, international organization designed by its founders to supervise and liberalize international trade. The organization officially commenced on 1 January 1995, under the Marrakesh Agreement, succeeding the 1947 General Agreement on Tariffs and Trade (GATT.)

The _____ deals with regulation of trade between participating countries; it provides a framework for negotiating and formalising trade agreements, and a dispute resolution process aimed at enforcing participants' adherence to _____ agreements which are signed by representatives of member governments and ratified by their parliaments.

a. 2009 G-20 London summit protests
b. Backus-Kehoe-Kydland consumption correlation puzzle
c. World Trade Organization
d. Bio-energy village

19. The _____ is a treaty of the World Trade Organization (WTO) that entered into force in January 1995 as a result of the Uruguay Round negotiations. The treaty was created to extend the multilateral trading system to service sector, in the same way the General Agreement on Tariffs and Trade (GATT) provides such a system for merchandise trade.

All members of the WTO are signatories to the GATS.

a. GATT
b. General Agreement on Tariffs and Trade
c. Dutch-Scandinavian Economic Pact
d. General Agreement on Trade in Services

20. _____ are legal property rights over creations of the mind, both artistic and commercial, and the corresponding fields of law. Under _____ law, owners are granted certain exclusive rights to a variety of intangible assets, such as musical, literary, and artistic works; ideas, discoveries and inventions; and words, phrases, symbols, and designs. Common types of _____ include copyrights, trademarks, patents, industrial design rights and trade secrets.

a. Independent contractor
b. Intellectual Property
c. Ease of Doing Business Index
d. Expedited Funds Availability Act

21. _____ is a term used to describe how different aspects between economies are integrated. The basics of this theory were written by the Hungarian Economist Béla Balassa in the 1960s. As _____ increases, the barriers of trade between markets diminishes.

a. Inward investment
b. Import license
c. Import
d. Economic Integration

22. _____ in economics and business is the result of an exchange and from that trade we assign a numerical monetary value to a good, service or asset. If Alice trades Bob 4 apples for an orange, the _____ of an orange is 4 apples. Inversely, the _____ of an apple is 1/4 oranges.

a. Price book
b. Premium pricing
c. Price war
d. Price

23. _____ exists when sales of identical goods or services are transacted at different prices from the same provider. In a theoretical market with perfect information, no transaction costs or prohibition on secondary exchange (or re-selling) to prevent arbitrage, _____ can only be a feature of monopoly and oligopoly markets, where market power can be exercised. Otherwise, the moment the seller tries to sell the same good at different prices, the buyer at the lower price can arbitrage by selling to the consumer buying at the higher price but with a tiny discount.

   a. Loss leader   b. Transfer pricing
   c. Lerner Index   d. Price discrimination

Chapter 9. Regional Economic Arrangements

1. A _____ is a customs union with common policies on product regulation, and freedom of movement of the factors of production (capital and labour) and of enterprise. The goal is that the movement of capital, labour, goods, and services between the members is as easy as within them. This is the fourth stage of economic integration.
   a. Competitiveness
   b. Grey market
   c. Mutual recognition agreement
   d. Common market

2. A _____ is a free trade area with a common external tariff. The participant countries set up common external trade policy, but in some cases they use different import quotas. Common competition policy is also helpful to avoid competition deficiency.
   a. Grey market
   b. Common market
   c. Bilateral Investment Treaty
   d. Customs Union

3. The _____ is a trilateral trade bloc in North America created by the governments of the United States, Canada, and Mexico. The agreement creating the trade bloc came into force on January 1, 1994. It superseded the Canada-United States Free Trade Agreement between the U.S. and Canada.
   a. Federal Reserve Bank Notes
   b. Demand-side technologies
   c. Case-Shiller Home Price Indices
   d. North American Free Trade Agreement

4. A _____ is a duty imposed on goods when they are moved across a political boundary. They are usually associated with protectionism, the economic policy of restraining trade between nations. For political reasons, _____s are usually imposed on imported goods, although they may also be imposed on exported goods.
   a. 1921 recession
   b. Tariff
   c. 100-year flood
   d. 130-30 fund

5. _____s is the social science that studies the production, distribution, and consumption of goods and services. The term _____s comes from the Ancient Greek οἰκονομία from οἶκος (oikos, 'house') + νόμος (nomos, 'custom' or 'law'), hence 'rules of the house(hold)'. Current _____ models developed out of the broader field of political economy in the late 19th century, owing to a desire to use an empirical approach more akin to the physical sciences.
   a. Opportunity cost
   b. Inflation
   c. Energy economics
   d. Economic

Chapter 9. Regional Economic Arrangements

6. A _____ is:

   - Rewrite _____, in generative grammar and computer science
   - Standardization, a formal and widely-accepted statement, fact, definition, or qualification
   - Operation, a determinate _____ for performing a mathematical operation and obtaining a certain result (Mathematics, Logic)
     - Unary operation
     - Binary operation
   - _____ of inference, a function from sets of formulae to formulae (Mathematics, Logic)
   - _____ of thumb, principle with broad application that is not intended to be strictly accurate or reliable for every situation. Also often simply referred to as a _____
   - Moral, an atomic element of a moral code for guiding choices in human behavior
   - Heuristic, a quantized '_____' which shows a tendency or probability for successful function
   - A regulation, as in sports
   - A Production _____, as in computer science
   - Procedural law, a _____ set governing the application of laws to cases
     - A law, which may informally be called a '_____'
     - A court ruling, a decision by a court
   - In the U.S. Government, a regulation mandated by Congress, but written or expanded upon by the Executive Branch.
   - Norm (sociology), an informal but widely accepted _____, concept, truth, definition, or qualification (social norms, legal norms, coding norms)
   - Norm (philosophy), a kind of sentence or a reason to act, feel or believe
   - 'Rulership' is the concept of governance by a government:
     - Military _____, governance by a military body
     - Monastic _____, a collection of precepts that guides the life of monks or nuns in a religious order where the superior holds the place of Christ
   - Slide _____

   - '_____,' a song by Ayumi Hamasaki
   - '_____,' a song by rapper Nas
   - '_____s,' an album by the band The Whitest Boy Alive
   - _____s: Pyaar Ka Superhit Formula, a 2003 Bollywood film
   - ruler, an instrument for measuring lengths
   - _____, a component of an astrolabe, circumferator or similar instrument
   - The _____s, a bestselling self-help book
   - _____ Project (Run Up-to-date Linux Everywhere), a project that aims to use up-to-date Linux software on old PCs
   - _____ engine, a software system that helps managing business _____s
   - Ja _____, a hip hop artist
     - R.U.L.E., a 2005 greatest hits album by rapper Ja _____
   - '_____s,' a KMFDM song

a. Technocracy
b. Rule
c. Procter ' Gamble
d. Demand

7. _____ describes a set of laws relating to domestic agriculture and imports of foreign agricultural products. Governments usually implement agricultural policies with the goal of achieving a specific outcome in the domestic agricultural product markets. Outcomes can involve, for example, a guaranteed supply level, price stability, product quality, product selection, land use or employment.
   a. ACCRA Cost of Living Index
   b. ACEA agreement
   c. Intercropping
   d. Agricultural Policy

8. The _____ is an economic and political union of 27 member states, located primarily in Europe. It was established by the Treaty of Maastricht on 1 November 1993, upon the foundations of the pre-existing European Economic Community. With a population of almost 500 million, the _____ generates an estimated 30% share (US$18.4 trillion in 2008) of the nominal gross world product.
   a. ACEA agreement
   b. European Court of Justice
   c. ACCRA Cost of Living Index
   d. European Union

9. _____ in its classic form is defined as a company from one country making a physical investment into building a factory in another country. It is the establishment of an enterprise by a foreigner. Its definition can be extended to include investments made to acquire lasting interest in enterprises operating outside of the economy of the investor.
   a. Federal Deposit Insurance Corporation
   b. Non-governmental organization
   c. Foreign direct investment
   d. Financial Stability Forum

10. The _____ are two of the treaties of the European Union signed on March 25, 1957. Both treaties were signed by The Six: Belgium, France, Italy, Luxembourg, the Netherlands and West Germany.

The first established the European Economic Community and the second established the European Atomic Energy Community (EAEC or Euratom.)

   a. 100-year flood
   b. Maastricht Treaty
   c. Treaties of Rome
   d. Treaty of Amsterdam

11. _____ is a type of trade policy that allows traders to act and transact without interference from government. Thus, the policy permits trading partners mutual gains from trade, with goods and services produced according to the theory of comparative advantage.

Under a _____ policy, prices are a reflection of true supply and demand, and are the sole determinant of resource allocation.

   a. 130-30 fund
   b. 100-year flood
   c. 1921 recession
   d. Free Trade

12. The _____ is the official currency of 16 of the 27 member states of the European Union (EU.) The states, known collectively as the Eurozone, are Austria, Belgium, Cyprus, Finland, France, Germany, Greece, Ireland, Italy, Luxembourg, Malta, the Netherlands, Portugal, Slovakia, Slovenia, and Spain. The currency is also used in a further five European countries, with and without formal agreements and is consequently used daily by some 327 million Europeans.
   a. Equity capital market
   b. Import and Export Price Indices
   c. IRS Code 3401
   d. Euro

13. _____ is sometimes referred to as _____, actually it means Economic Monetary Union.

First ideas of an economic and monetary union in Europe were raised well before establishing the European Communities. For example, already in the League of Nations, Gustav Stresemann asked in 1929 for a European currency (Link) against the background of an increased economic division due to a number of new nation states in Europe after WWI.

  a. European Monetary Union
  b. Euro Interbank Offered Rate
  c. European Monetary System
  d. Exchange rate mechanism

14. The _____ was signed on 7 February 1992 in Maastricht, the Netherlands after final negotiations on 9 December 1991 between the members of the European Community and entered into force on 1 November 1993 during the Delors Commission. It created the European Union and led to the creation of the euro. The _____ has been amended to a degree by later treaties.

  a. Maastricht Treaty
  b. Treaties of Rome
  c. Treaty of Amsterdam
  d. 100-year flood

15. An economic and _____ is a single market with a common currency. It is to be distinguished from a mere currency union, which does not involve a single market. This is the fifth stage of economic integration.

  a. Commercial invoice
  b. Customs union
  c. Free trade zone
  d. Monetary Union

16. The _____ was a unilateral and temporary United States program initiated by the 1983 'Caribbean Basin Economic Recovery Act' (CBERA.) The _____ came into effect on January 1, 1984 and aimed to provide several tariff and trade benefits to many Central American and Caribbean countries. It arose in the context of a U.S. desire to respond with aid and trade to leftist movements that were active in some countries of the region, such as the guerrillas in El Salvador and the Sandinista government in Nicaragua.

  a. 100-year flood
  b. Caribbean Basin Initiative
  c. 1921 recession
  d. 130-30 fund

17. The _____ is a formal system of exemption from the more general rules of the World Trade Organization (WTO), (formerly, the General Agreement on Tariffs and Trade or GATT.) Specifically, it's a system of exemption from the Most Favored Nation principle (MFN) that obligates WTO member countries to treat the imports of all other WTO member countries no worse than they treat the imports of their 'most favored' trading partner. In essence, MFN requires WTO member countries to treat imports coming from all other WTO member countries equally, that is, by imposing equal tariffs on them, etc.

  a. Corn Laws
  b. Nature of the Firm
  c. Misappropriation
  d. Generalized System of Preferences

18. The _____ or gross domestic income (GDI), a basic measure of an economy's economic performance, is the market value of all final goods and services produced within the borders of a nation in a year. _____ can be defined in three ways, all of which are conceptually identical. First, it is equal to the total expenditures for all final goods and services produced within the country in a stipulated period of time (usually a 365-day year.)

  a. Gross domestic product
  b. Market structure
  c. Countercyclical
  d. Monopolistic competition

Chapter 9. Regional Economic Arrangements

19. _____ is a Regional Trade Agreement among Argentina, Brazil, Paraguay and Uruguay founded in 1991 by the Treaty of Asunci>ón, which was later amended and updated by the 1994 Treaty of Ouro Preto. Its purpose is to promote free trade and the fluid movement of goods, people, and currency.

_____ origins trace back to 1985 when Presidents Ra>úl Alfons>ín of Argentina and Jos>é Sarney of Brazil signed the Argentina-Brazil Integration and Economics Cooperation Program or PICE .

a. 130-30 fund
b. MERCOSUR
c. Free trade area
d. 100-year flood

20. _____ is a term in international relations that refers to multiple countries working in concert on a given issue.

Most international organizations, such as the United Nations (UN) and the World Trade Organization are multilateral in nature. The main proponents of _____ have traditionally been the middle powers such as Canada, Australia and the Nordic countries.

a. Multilateralism
b. Simultaneous policy
c. Global governance
d. 100-year flood

21. _____ is a term used to describe how different aspects between economies are integrated. The basics of this theory were written by the Hungarian Economist Béla Balassa in the 1960s. As _____ increases, the barriers of trade between markets diminishes.

a. Import license
b. Economic Integration
c. Inward investment
d. Import

22. The term '_____' refers to the concept of collecting information and attempting to spot a pattern in the information. In some fields of study, the term '_____' has more formally-defined meanings.

In project management _____ is a mathematical technique that uses historical results to predict future outcome.

a. Quantile regression
b. Trend analysis
c. Coefficient of determination
d. Probit model

Chapter 10. International Trade and Economic Growth

1. _____s is the social science that studies the production, distribution, and consumption of goods and services. The term _____s comes from the Ancient Greek οá¼°κονομῖα from οá¼¶κος (oikos, 'house') + vΐŒμος (nomos, 'custom' or 'law'), hence 'rules of the house(hold)'. Current _____ models developed out of the broader field of political economy in the late 19th century, owing to a desire to use an empirical approach more akin to the physical sciences.

   a. Energy economics
   b. Opportunity cost
   c. Inflation
   d. Economic

2. _____ is the development of economic wealth of countries or regions for the well-being of their inhabitants. It is the process by which a nation improves the economic, political, and social well being of its people. From a policy perspective, _____ can be defined as efforts that seek to improve the economic well-being and quality of life for a community by creating and/or retaining jobs and supporting or growing incomes and the tax base.

   a. Inflation
   b. Experimental economics
   c. Economic development
   d. Economic methodology

3. The _____ or gross domestic income (GDI), a basic measure of an economy's economic performance, is the market value of all final goods and services produced within the borders of a nation in a year. _____ can be defined in three ways, all of which are conceptually identical. First, it is equal to the total expenditures for all final goods and services produced within the country in a stipulated period of time (usually a 365-day year.)

   a. Monopolistic competition
   b. Market structure
   c. Countercyclical
   d. Gross domestic product

4. _____ is a misspelled phrase from Latin 'pro capite' phrase meaning per head with pro meaning 'per' or 'for each' and capite meaning 'head.' Both words together equate to the phrase 'for each head.'

   It is usually used in the field of statistics to indicate the average per person for any given concern, such as income, crime rate, etc.

   It is also used in wills to indicate that each of the named beneficiaries should receive, by devise or bequest, equal shares of the estate. This is in contrast to a per stirpes division, in which each branch of the inheriting family inherits an equal share of the estate.

   a. Sargan test
   b. Per capita
   c. False positive rate
   d. Population statistics

5. _____ is the change in population over time, and can be quantified as the change in the number of individuals in a population using 'per unit time' for measurement. The term _____ can technically refer to any species, but almost always refers to humans, and it is often used informally for the more specific demographic term _____ rate , and is often used to refer specifically to the growth of the population of the world.

   Simple models of _____ include the Malthusian Growth Model and the logistic model.

   a. 130-30 fund
   b. Population growth
   c. Population dynamics
   d. 100-year flood

Chapter 10. International Trade and Economic Growth

6. _____ is the increase in the amount of the goods and services produced by an economy over time. It is conventionally measured as the percent rate of increase in real gross domestic product, or real GDP. Growth is usually calculated in real terms, i.e. inflation-adjusted terms, in order to net out the effect of inflation on the price of the goods and services produced.
   a. ACEA agreement
   b. ACCRA Cost of Living Index
   c. AD-IA Model
   d. Economic growth

7. In economics, _____ are the resources employed to produce goods and services. They facilitate production but do not become part of the product (as with raw materials) or significantly transformed by the production process (as with fuel used to power machinery.) To 19th century economists, the _____ were land (natural resources, gifts from nature), labor (the ability to work), and capital goods (human-made tools and equipment.)
   a. Factors of production
   b. Product Pipeline
   c. Long-run
   d. Hicks-neutral technical change

8. In economics, _____ is the total supply of goods and services produced by a national economy during a specific time period. It is the total amount of goods and services in the economy available at all possible price levels.
   a. Aggregate supply
   b. Aggregate demand
   c. Aggregate expenditure
   d. Aggregation problem

9. _____ is a type of private equity investment, most often a minority investment, in relatively mature companies that are looking for capital to expand or restructure operations, enter new markets or finance a significant acquisition without a change of control of the business.

Companies that seek _____, will often do so in order to finance a transformational event in their lifecycle. These companies are likely to be more mature than venture capital funded companies, able to generate revenue and operating profits but unable to generate sufficient cash to fund major expansions, acquisitions or other investments.

   a. Growth capital
   b. Club deal
   c. Startup company
   d. Seed money

10. In microeconomics, _____ is quite simply the conversion of inputs into outputs. It is an economic process that uses resources to create a good or service that is suitable for exchange. This can include manufacturing, storing, shipping, and packaging.
    a. Solved
    b. Production
    c. MET
    d. Red Guards

11. In economics, a _____ is a function that specifies the output of a firm, an industry, or an entire economy for all combinations of inputs. A meta-_____ compares the practice of the existing entities converting inputs X into output y to determine the most efficient practice _____ of the existing entities, whether the most efficient feasible practice production or the most efficient actual practice production. In either case, the maximum output of a technologically-determined production process is a mathematical function of input factors of production.
    a. Constant elasticity of substitution
    b. Post-Fordism
    c. Short-run
    d. Production function

Chapter 10. International Trade and Economic Growth

12. _____ in its classic form is defined as a company from one country making a physical investment into building a factory in another country. It is the establishment of an enterprise by a foreigner. Its definition can be extended to include investments made to acquire lasting interest in enterprises operating outside of the economy of the investor.

   a. Financial Stability Forum
   b. Federal Deposit Insurance Corporation
   c. Foreign Direct Investment
   d. Non-governmental organization

13. A _____ or transnational corporation is a corporation or enterprise that manages production or delivers services in more than one country. It can also be referred to as an international corporation.

   The first modern MNC is generally thought to be the Dutch East India Company, established in 1602.

   a. Multinational corporation
   b. Foreign direct investment
   c. Luxembourg Income Study
   d. Rakon

14. In economics, _____ (TFP) is a variable which accounts for effects in total output not caused by inputs. For example, a year with unusually good weather will tend to have higher output, because bad weather hinders agricultural output. A variable like weather does not directly relate to unit inputs, so weather is considered a _____ variable.

   a. 35-hour working week
   b. Human rights
   c. Flow to Equity-Approach
   d. Total-factor productivity

15. The _____ consists of a number of economic theories which describe the nature of the firm, company including its existence, its behaviour, and its relationship with the market.

   In simplified terms, the _____ aims to answer these questions:

   1. Existence - why do firms emerge, why are not all transactions in the economy mediated over the market?
   2. Boundaries - why the boundary between firms and the market is located exactly there? Which transactions are performed internally and which are negotiated on the market?
   3. Organization - why are firms structured in such specific way? What is the interplay of formal and informal relationships?

   Despite looking simple, these questions are not answered by the established economic theory, which usually views firms as given, and treats them as black boxes without any internal structure.

   The First World War period saw a change of emphasis in economic theory away from industry-level analysis which mainly included analysing markets to analysis at the level of the firm, as it became increasingly clear that perfect competition was no longer an adequate model of how firms behaved. Economic theory till then had focussed on trying to understand markets alone and there had been little study on understanding why firms or organisations exist.

   a. Theory of the firm
   b. Technology gap
   c. Policy Ineffectiveness Proposition
   d. Khazzoom-Brookes postulate

Chapter 10. International Trade and Economic Growth

16. _____ in economics refers to metrics and measures of output from production processes, per unit of input. Labor _____, for example, is typically measured as a ratio of output per labor-hour, an input. _____ may be conceived of as a metrics of the technical or engineering efficiency of production.
   a. Piece work
   b. Fordism
   c. Production-possibility frontier
   d. Productivity

17. _____ is the process of sharing of skills, knowledge, technologies, methods of manufacturing, samples of manufacturing and facilities among governments and other institutions to ensure that scientific and technological developments are accessible to a wider range of users who can then further develop and exploit the technology into new products, processes, applications, materials or services. It is closely related to (and may arguably be considered a subset of) Knowledge transfer. Related terms, used almost synonymously, include 'technology valorisation' and 'technology commercialisation'.
   a. Patent
   b. Law of increasing relative cost
   c. Judgment summons
   d. Technology transfer

18. _____ is an economic concept that tries to explain the apparent relationship between the exploitation of natural resources and a decline in the manufacturing sector combined with moral fallout. The theory is that an increase in revenues from natural resources will deindustrialise a natione;s economy by raising the exchange rate, which makes the manufacturing sector less competitive and public services entangled with business interests. However, it is extremely difficult to definitively say that _____ is the cause of the decreasing manufacturing sector, since there are many other factors at play in the very complex global economy.
   a. Gravity model of trade
   b. Dutch disease
   c. Triffin dilemma
   d. Comparative advantage

19. The primary sector of the economy involves changing natural resources into _____. Most products from this sector are considered raw materials for other industries. Major businesses in this sector include agriculture, agribusiness, fishing, forestry and all mining and quarrying industries.
   a. Private sector
   b. Tertiary sector of economy
   c. Primary products
   d. Secondary sector of the economy

20. _____ was the first United States Secretary of the Treasury, a Founding Father, economist, and political philosopher. He led calls for the Philadelphia Convention, was one of America's first Constitutional lawyers, and cowrote the Federalist Papers, a primary source for Constitutional interpretation.

Born on the British West Indian island of Nevis, Hamilton was educated in the Thirteen Colonies.

   a. Adam Smith
   b. Alexander Hamilton
   c. American exceptionalism
   d. Economic impact of immigration

21. In economics, an _____ is any good (e.g. a commodity) or service brought into one country from another country in a legitimate fashion, typically for use in trade.It is a good that is brought in from another country for sale. _____ goods or services are provided to domestic consumers by foreign producers. An _____ in the receiving country is an export to the sending country.
   a. Incoterms
   b. Import
   c. Economic integration
   d. Import quota

Chapter 10. International Trade and Economic Growth

22. _____ industrialization is a trade and economic policy based on the premise that a country should attempt to reduce its foreign dependency through the local production of industrialized products. Adopted in many Latin American countries from the 1930s until the late 1980s, and in some Asian and African countries from the 1950s on, Import substitutionI was theoretically organized in the works of Raúl Prebisch, Hans Singer, Celso Furtado and other structural economic thinkers, and gained prominence with the creation of the United Nations Economic Commission for Latin America and the Caribbean . Insofar as its suggestion of state-induced industrialization through governmental spending, it is largely influenced by Keynesian thinking, as well as the infant industry arguments adopted by some highly industrialized countries, such as the United States, until the 1940s.
   a. ACEA agreement
   b. AD-IA Model
   c. ACCRA Cost of Living Index
   d. Import Substitution

23. _____ in economics and business is the result of an exchange and from that trade we assign a numerical monetary value to a good, service or asset. If Alice trades Bob 4 apples for an orange, the _____ of an orange is 4 apples. Inversely, the _____ of an apple is 1/4 oranges.
   a. Premium pricing
   b. Price war
   c. Price book
   d. Price

24. In economics a country's _____ is commonly understood as the amount of land, labor, capital, and entrepreneurship that a country possesses and can exploit for manufacturing. Countries with a large endowment of resources tend to be more prosperous than those with a small endowment, all other things being equal. The development of sound institutions to access and equitably distribute these resources, however, is necessary in order for a country to obtain the greatest benefit from its _____.
   a. Factor endowment
   b. Dutch disease
   c. Price scissors
   d. Foreign Affiliate Trade Statistics

25. In economics, an _____ is any good or commodity, transported from one country to another country in a legitimate fashion, typically for use in trade. _____ goods or services are provided to foreign consumers by domestic producers. _____ is an important part of international trade.
   a. Export
   b. ACCRA Cost of Living Index
   c. AD-IA Model
   d. ACEA agreement

26. _____ is a statistic compiled by the Development Assistance Committee of the Organisation for Economic Co-operation and Development to measure aid. The DAC first compiled the statistic in 1969. It is widely used by academics and journalists as a convenient indicator of international aid flow.
   a. Untied aid
   b. International Finance Corporation
   c. International Finance Facility
   d. Official Development Assistance

27. The _____ is an international financial institution that provides financial and technical assistance to developing countries for development programs (e.g. bridges, roads, schools, etc.) with the stated goal of reducing poverty.

The _____ differs from the _____ Group, in that the _____ comprises only two institutions:

- International Bank for Reconstruction and Development (IBRD)
- International Development Association (IDA)

Chapter 10. International Trade and Economic Growth

Whereas the latter incorporates these two in addition to three more:

- International Finance Corporation (IFC)
- Multilateral Investment Guarantee Agency (MIGA)
- International Centre for Settlement of Investment Disputes (ICSID)

John Maynard Keynes (right) represented the UK at the conference, and Harry Dexter White represented the US.

The _____ is one of two major financial institutions created as a result of the Bretton Woods Conference in 1944. The International Monetary Fund, a related but separate institution, is the second.

a. Bank-State-Branch
b. Flow to Equity-Approach
c. Financial costs of the 2003 Iraq War
d. World Bank

28. The _____ was established in 1964 as a permanent intergovernmental body. It is the principal organ of the United Nations General Assembly dealing with trade, investment and development issues.

The organization's goals are to 'maximize the trade, investment and development opportunities of developing countries and assist them in their efforts to integrate into the world economy on an equitable basis.' (from official website.)

a. Our Global Neighborhood
b. International Standards of Accounting and Reporting
c. International Trade Centre
d. United Nations Conference on Trade and Development

29. The _____ , French/Spanish acronym ONUDI, is a specialized agency in the United Nations system, headquartered in Vienna, Austria. The Organization's primary objective is the promotion and acceleration of industrial development in developing countries and countries with economies in transition and the promotion of international industrial cooperation.

_____ believes that competitive and environmentally sustainable industry has a crucial role to play in accelerating economic growth, reducing poverty and achieving the Millennium Development Goals.

a. United Nations Industrial Development Organization
b. International Trade Centre
c. United Nations Development Programme
d. United Nations Conference on Trade and Development

Chapter 11. National Income Accounting and the Balance of Payments

1. The _____ or gross domestic income (GDI), a basic measure of an economy's economic performance, is the market value of all final goods and services produced within the borders of a nation in a year. _____ can be defined in three ways, all of which are conceptually identical. First, it is equal to the total expenditures for all final goods and services produced within the country in a stipulated period of time (usually a 365-day year.)
   a. Monopolistic competition
   b. Countercyclical
   c. Market structure
   d. Gross Domestic Product

2. A variety of measures of _____ and output are used in economics to estimate total economic activity in a country or region, including gross domestic product (GDP), gross national product (GNP), and net _____

   There are three main ways of calculating these numbers; the output approach, the income approach and the expenditure approach. In theory, the three must yield the same, because total expenditures on goods and services must equal the total income paid to the producers (Gnational income), and that must also equal the total value of the output of goods and services (GNP.)

   a. GNI per capita
   b. Volume index
   c. National income
   d. Gross world product

3. In economics, _____ is the total demand for final goods and services in the economy (Y) at a given time and price level. It is the amount of goods and services in the economy that will be purchased at all possible price levels. This is the demand for the gross domestic product of a country when inventory levels are static.
   a. Aggregation problem
   b. Aggregate supply
   c. Aggregate demand
   d. Aggregate expenditure

4. Economics:

   - _____ ,the desire to own something and the ability to pay for it
   - _____ curve, a graphic representation of a _____ schedule
   - _____ deposit, the money in checking accounts
   - _____ pull theory, the theory that inflation occurs when _____ for goods and services exceeds existing supplies
   - _____ schedule, a table that lists the quantity of a good a person will buy it each different price
   - _____ side economics, the school of economics at believes government spending and tax cuts open economy by raising _____

   a. McKesson ' Robbins scandal
   b. Variability
   c. Demand
   d. Production

5. _____ is a common concept in economics, and gives rise to derived concepts such as consumer debt. Generally _____ is defined by opposition to production. But the precise definition can vary because different schools of economists define production quite differently.
   a. Foreclosure data providers
   b. Cash or share options
   c. Federal Reserve Bank Notes
   d. Consumption

Chapter 11. National Income Accounting and the Balance of Payments 53

6. An _____, in economics, is the amount by which the real Gross domestic product exceeds potential GDP. The real GDP is also known as GDP 'adjusted for inflation', 'constant prices' GDP or 'constant dollar' GDP, because it measures the aggregate output in a country's income accounts in a given year, expressed in base-year prices. On the other hand, the potential GDP is the quantity of real GDP when a country's economy is at full-employment.
- a. ACCRA Cost of Living Index
- b. ACEA agreement
- c. Inflationary gap
- d. AD-IA Model

7. _____ in economics and business is the result of an exchange and from that trade we assign a numerical monetary value to a good, service or asset. If Alice trades Bob 4 apples for an orange, the _____ of an orange is 4 apples. Inversely, the _____ of an apple is 1/4 oranges.
- a. Premium pricing
- b. Price war
- c. Price book
- d. Price

8. An autarky is an economy that is self-sufficient and does not take part in international trade, or severely limits trade with the outside world. Likewise the term refers to an ecosystem not affected by influences from the outside, which relies entirely on its own resources. In the economic meaning, it is also referred to as a _____.
- a. Digital economy
- b. Transition economy
- c. Network Economy
- d. Closed economy

9. _____ describes a set of laws relating to domestic agriculture and imports of foreign agricultural products. Governments usually implement agricultural policies with the goal of achieving a specific outcome in the domestic agricultural product markets. Outcomes can involve, for example, a guaranteed supply level, price stability, product quality, product selection, land use or employment.
- a. ACCRA Cost of Living Index
- b. Intercropping
- c. ACEA agreement
- d. Agricultural Policy

10. In economics, the _____ measures the payments that flow between any individual country and all other countries. It is used to summarize all international economic transactions for that country during a specific time period, usually a year. The _____ is determined by the country's exports and imports of goods, services, and financial capital, as well as financial transfers.
- a. Balance of payments
- b. Gross domestic product per barrel
- c. Gross world product
- d. Skyscraper Index

11. The _____ is an economic and political union of 27 member states, located primarily in Europe. It was established by the Treaty of Maastricht on 1 November 1993, upon the foundations of the pre-existing European Economic Community. With a population of almost 500 million, the _____ generates an estimated 30% share (US$18.4 trillion in 2008) of the nominal gross world product.
- a. ACCRA Cost of Living Index
- b. European Court of Justice
- c. ACEA agreement
- d. European Union

12. The _____ was signed on 7 February 1992 in Maastricht, the Netherlands after final negotiations on 9 December 1991 between the members of the European Community and entered into force on 1 November 1993 during the Delors Commission. It created the European Union and led to the creation of the euro. The _____ has been amended to a degree by later treaties.

Chapter 11. National Income Accounting and the Balance of Payments

a. Treaties of Rome
b. Maastricht Treaty
c. Treaty of Amsterdam
d. 100-year flood

13. A _____ is the transfer of wealth from one party (such as a person or company) to another. A _____ is usually made in exchange for the provision of goods, services or both, or to fulfill a legal obligation.

The simplest and oldest form of _____ is barter, the exchange of one good or service for another.

a. Soft count
b. Social gravity
c. Going concern
d. Payment

14. A _____ is an expression that compares quantities relative to each other. The most common examples involve two quantities, but any number of quantities can be compared. _____s are represented mathematically by separating each quantity with a colon, for example the _____ 2:3, which is read as the _____ 'two to three'.

a. Y-intercept
b. Ratio
c. 130-30 fund
d. 100-year flood

15. In financial accounting, the _____ is one of the accounts in shareholders' equity. Sole proprietorships have a single _____ in the owner's equity. Partnerships maintain a _____ for each of the partners.

a. Compensation of employees
b. Capital account
c. Net national product
d. Current account

16. In economics, the _____ is one of the two primary components of the balance of payments, the other being the capital account. It is the sum of the balance of trade (exports minus imports of goods and services), net factor income (such as interest and dividends) and net transfer payments (such as foreign aid.)

$$\begin{aligned}\text{Current account} = &\text{ Balance of trade} \\ &+ \text{Net factor income from abroad} \\ &+ \text{Net unilateral transfers from abroad}\end{aligned}$$

The _____ balance is one of two major metrics of the nature of a country's foreign trade (the other being the net capital outflow.)

a. Current account
b. Compensation of employees
c. National Income and Product Accounts
d. Gross private domestic investment

17. A _____ is an object whose consumption increases the utility of the consumer, for which the quantity demanded exceeds the quantity supplied at zero price. _____s are usually modeled as having diminishing marginal utility. The first individual purchase has high utility; the second has less.

a. Merit good
b. Good
c. Pie method
d. Composite good

18. In economics, economic output is divided into physical goods and intangible services. Consumption of _____ is assumed to produce utility. It is often used when referring to a _____ Tax.

Chapter 11. National Income Accounting and the Balance of Payments

a. Private good
c. Manufactured goods
b. Composite good
d. Goods and services

19. In business and accounting, _____ are everything of value that is owned by a person or company. It is a claim on the property your income of a borrower. The balance sheet of a firm records the monetary value of the _____ owned by the firm.
   a. Amortization schedule
   c. ACEA agreement
   b. Assets
   d. ACCRA Cost of Living Index

20. In economics, an _____ is any good or commodity, transported from one country to another country in a legitimate fashion, typically for use in trade. _____ goods or services are provided to foreign consumers by domestic producers. _____ is an important part of international trade.
   a. Export
   c. ACCRA Cost of Living Index
   b. AD-IA Model
   d. ACEA agreement

21. The _____ is an international organization that oversees the global financial system by following the macroeconomic policies of its member countries, in particular those with an impact on exchange rates and the balance of payments. It is an organization formed to stabilize international exchange rates and facilitate development. It also offers financial and technical assistance to its members, making it an international lender of last resort.
   a. International Monetary Fund
   c. ACEA agreement
   b. Office of Thrift Supervision
   d. ACCRA Cost of Living Index

22. _____ are potential claims on the freely usable currencies of International Monetary Fund members. _____s have the ISO 4217 currency code XDR.

_____s are defined in terms of a basket of major currencies used in international trade and finance.

   a. Special drawing rights
   c. Quota share
   b. Metzler paradox
   d. Bilateral Investment Treaty

23. A country's _____ is a financial statement setting out the value and composition of that country's external financial assets and liabilities.

The difference between a country's external financial assets and liabilities is the net _____

_____ = domestically owned foreign assets - foreign owned domestic assets

   a. Overshooting model
   c. Optimum currency area
   b. International investment position
   d. International finance

24. _____s is the social science that studies the production, distribution, and consumption of goods and services. The term _____s comes from the Ancient Greek οἰκονομία from οἶκος (oikos, 'house') + νόμος (nomos, 'custom' or 'law'), hence 'rules of the house(hold)'. Current _____ models developed out of the broader field of political economy in the late 19th century, owing to a desire to use an empirical approach more akin to the physical sciences.

a. Energy economics
b. Opportunity cost
c. Inflation
d. Economic

25. The term '_____' refers to the concept of collecting information and attempting to spot a pattern in the information. In some fields of study, the term '_____' has more formally-defined meanings.

In project management _____ is a mathematical technique that uses historical results to predict future outcome.

a. Coefficient of determination
b. Quantile regression
c. Trend analysis
d. Probit model

Chapter 12. International Transactions and Financial Markets

1. The _____ is where currency trading takes place. It is where banks and other official institutions facilitate the buying and selling of foreign currencies. FX transactions typically involve one party purchasing a quantity of one currency in exchange for paying a quantity of another.
   a. Currency swap
   b. Floating currency
   c. Foreign exchange market
   d. Covered interest arbitrage

2. In finance, the _____s between two currencies specifies how much one currency is worth in terms of the other. It is the value of a foreign natione;s currency in terms of the home natione;s currency. For example an _____ of 102 Japanese yen to the United States dollar means that JPY 102 is worth the same as USD 1.
   a. ACEA agreement
   b. Interbank market
   c. Exchange rate
   d. ACCRA Cost of Living Index

3. In economics, an _____ is any good or commodity, transported from one country to another country in a legitimate fashion, typically for use in trade. _____ goods or services are provided to foreign consumers by domestic producers. _____ is an important part of international trade.
   a. AD-IA Model
   b. ACEA agreement
   c. ACCRA Cost of Living Index
   d. Export

4. In economics, an _____ is any good (e.g. a commodity) or service brought into one country from another country in a legitimate fashion, typically for use in trade.It is a good that is brought in from another country for sale. _____ goods or services are provided to domestic consumers by foreign producers. An _____ in the receiving country is an export to the sending country.
   a. Incoterms
   b. Economic integration
   c. Import quota
   d. Import

5. A standard, commercial _____ is a document issued mostly by a financial institution, used primarily in trade finance, which usually provides an irrevocable payment undertaking.

   The LC can also be the source of payment for a transaction, meaning that redeeming the _____ will pay an exporter. Letters of credit are used primarily in international trade transactions of significant value, for deals between a supplier in one country and a customer in another.

   a. Celler-Kefauver Act
   b. Contract theory
   c. Patent misuse
   d. Letter of credit

6. In economics, _____ is the total demand for final goods and services in the economy (Y) at a given time and price level. It is the amount of goods and services in the economy that will be purchased at all possible price levels. This is the demand for the gross domestic product of a country when inventory levels are static.
   a. Aggregate expenditure
   b. Aggregation problem
   c. Aggregate supply
   d. Aggregate demand

7. A _____ refers to any type debt instrument, such as a loan, bond, mortgage that does not have a fixed rate of interest over the life of the instrument. Such debt typically uses an index or other base rate for establishing the interest rate for each relevant period. One of the most common rates to use as the basis for applying interest rates is the London Inter-bank Offered Rate, or LIBOR

a. Money market
c. Disposal tax effect
b. Moneylender
d. Floating interest rate

8. Economics:

- _____, the desire to own something and the ability to pay for it
- _____ curve, a graphic representation of a _____ schedule
- _____ deposit, the money in checking accounts
- _____ pull theory, the theory that inflation occurs when _____ for goods and services exceeds existing supplies
- _____ schedule, a table that lists the quantity of a good a person will buy it each different price
- _____ side economics, the school of economics at believes government spending and tax cuts open economy by raising _____

a. McKesson ' Robbins scandal
c. Production
b. Variability
d. Demand

9. A _____ is the transfer of wealth from one party (such as a person or company) to another. A _____ is usually made in exchange for the provision of goods, services or both, or to fulfill a legal obligation.

The simplest and oldest form of _____ is barter, the exchange of one good or service for another.

a. Going concern
c. Soft count
b. Social gravity
d. Payment

10. _____ is money accepted for exchange of goods in an economy. The prevalence of one money over another arises, usually, when a government designates through decrees that the government shall accept only particular notes and coins in payment for taxes. Typically, money of _____ consists of stamped coins and minted paper bills.

a. Totnes pound
c. Currency
b. Security thread
d. Local currency

11. A _____ is a foreign exchange agreement between two parties to exchange principal and fixed rate interest payments on a loan in one currency for principal and fixed rate interest payments on an equal (regarding net present value) loan in another currency. _____s are motivated by comparative advantage. _____s were introduced by the World Bank in 1981 to obtain Swiss franks and German marks by exchanging cash flows with IBM.

a. Foreign exchange spot trading
c. Strong dollar policy
b. Currency Swap
d. Non-deliverable forward

12. In finance, a _____ is a standardized contract, to buy or sell a specified commodity of standardized quality at a certain date in the future, at a market determined price (the futures price.)

The price is determined by the instantaneous equilibrium between the forces of supply and demand among competing buy and sell orders on the exchange at the time of the purchase or sale of the contract.

In many cases, the items may be such non-traditional 'commodities' as foreign currencies, commercial or government paper [e.g., bonds], or 'baskets' of corporate equity ['stock indices'] or other financial instruments.

a. Power reverse dual currency note
b. Local volatility
c. Futures contract
d. Dual currency deposit

13. _____ involves the 'matching' of lenders with savings to borrowers who need money by an agent or third party, such as a bank.

If this matching is successful, the lender obtains a positive rate of return, the borrower receives a return for risk taking and entrepeneurship and the banker receives a marginal return for making the successful match. If the borrower's speculative play with the depositor's funds does not pay off, the depositor can lose the savings borrowed by the borrower and the bank can face significant losses on its loan portfolio.

a. Intermediation
b. Arranger
c. Annual percentage rate
d. Origination fee

14. The _____ is the market for securities, where companies and governments can raise longterm funds. It is a market in which money is lent for periods longer than a year. The _____ includes the stock market and the bond market.

a. Capital market
b. Multi-family office
c. Financial instrument
d. Performance attribution

15. In finance, the _____ is the global financial market for short-term borrowing and lending. It provides short-term liquidity funding for the global financial system. The _____ is where short-term obligations such as Treasury bills, commercial paper and bankers' acceptances are bought and sold.

a. Consignment stock
b. Deferred compensation
c. Money market
d. T-Model

16. In economic models, the _____ time frame assumes no fixed factors of production. Firms can enter or leave the marketplace, and the cost (and availability) of land, labor, raw materials, and capital goods can be assumed to vary. In contrast, in the short-run time frame, certain factors are assumed to be fixed, because there is not sufficient time for them to change.

a. Price/performance ratio
b. Diseconomies of scale
c. Productivity world
d. Long-run

17. In economics, the concept of the _____ refers to the decision-making time frame of a firm in which at least one factor of production is fixed. Costs which are fixed in the _____ have no impact on a firms decisions. For example a firm can raise output by increasing the amount of labour through overtime.

a. Hicks-neutral technical change
b. Short-run
c. Product Pipeline
d. Productivity model

18. In economics, a _____ is a mechanism that allows people to easily buy and sell (trade) financial securities (such as stocks and bonds), commodities (such as precious metals or agricultural goods), and other fungible items of value at low transaction costs and at prices that reflect the efficient-market hypothesis.

_____s have evolved significantly over several hundred years and are undergoing constant innovation to improve liquidity.

Both general markets (where many commodities are traded) and specialized markets (where only one commodity is traded) exist.

a. Convertible arbitrage
c. Market anomaly

b. Financial Market
d. Noise trader

19.

A _____ is a type of financial intermediary and a type of bank. Commercial banking is also known as business banking. It is a bank that provides checking accounts, savings accounts, and money market accounts and that accepts time deposits.

a. Lombard banking
c. Bought deal

b. Commercial bank
d. Daylight overdraft

20. The _____ consists of a number of economic theories which describe the nature of the firm, company including its existence, its behaviour, and its relationship with the market.

In simplified terms, the _____ aims to answer these questions:

1. Existence - why do firms emerge, why are not all transactions in the economy mediated over the market?
2. Boundaries - why the boundary between firms and the market is located exactly there? Which transactions are performed internally and which are negotiated on the market?
3. Organization - why are firms structured in such specific way? What is the interplay of formal and informal relationships?

Despite looking simple, these questions are not answered by the established economic theory, which usually views firms as given, and treats them as black boxes without any internal structure.

The First World War period saw a change of emphasis in economic theory away from industry-level analysis which mainly included analysing markets to analysis at the level of the firm, as it became increasingly clear that perfect competition was no longer an adequate model of how firms behaved. Economic theory till then had focussed on trying to understand markets alone and there had been little study on understanding why firms or organisations exist.

a. Khazzoom-Brookes postulate
c. Policy Ineffectiveness Proposition

b. Theory of the firm
d. Technology gap

Chapter 12. International Transactions and Financial Markets

21. Market _____ is a business, economics or investment term that refers to an asset's ability to be easily converted through an act of buying or selling without causing a significant movement in the price and with minimum loss of value. Money, or cash on hand, is the most liquid asset. An act of exchange of a less liquid asset with a more liquid asset is called liquidation.
    a. Liquidity
    b. 100-year flood
    c. 1921 recession
    d. 130-30 fund

22. _____s are deposits denominated in US dollars at banks outside the United States, and thus are not under the jurisdiction of the Federal Reserve. Consequently, such deposits are subject to much less regulation than similar deposits within the United States, allowing for higher margins. There is nothing 'European' about _____ deposits; a US dollar-denominated deposit in Tokyo or Caracas would likewise be deemed _____ deposits.
    a. ACEA agreement
    b. AD-IA Model
    c. Eurodollar
    d. ACCRA Cost of Living Index

23. _____s is the social science that studies the production, distribution, and consumption of goods and services. The term _____s comes from the Ancient Greek οἰκονομία from οἶκος (oikos, 'house') + νόμος (nomos, 'custom' or 'law'), hence 'rules of the house(hold)'. Current _____ models developed out of the broader field of political economy in the late 19th century, owing to a desire to use an empirical approach more akin to the physical sciences.
    a. Energy economics
    b. Inflation
    c. Opportunity cost
    d. Economic

24. The _____ was established in 1964 as a permanent intergovernmental body. It is the principal organ of the United Nations General Assembly dealing with trade, investment and development issues.

The organization's goals are to 'maximize the trade, investment and development opportunities of developing countries and assist them in their efforts to integrate into the world economy on an equitable basis.' (from official website.)

   a. Our Global Neighborhood
   b. International Standards of Accounting and Reporting
   c. International Trade Centre
   d. United Nations Conference on Trade and Development

Chapter 13. Exchange Rates and Their Determination: A Basic Model

1. _____ is a term used in accounting relating to the increase in value of an asset. In this sense it is the reverse of depreciation, which measures the fall in value of assets over their normal life-time.

_____ is a rise of a currency in a floating exchange rate.

a. AD-IA Model
b. ACEA agreement
c. ACCRA Cost of Living Index
d. Appreciation

2. _____ is a term used in accounting, economics and finance to spread the cost of an asset over the span of several years.

In simple words we can say that _____ is the reduction in the value of an asset due to usage, passage of time, wear and tear, technological outdating or obsolescence, depletion, inadequacy, rot, rust, decay or other such factors.

In accounting, _____ is a term used to describe any method of attributing the historical or purchase cost of an asset across its useful life, roughly corresponding to normal wear and tear.

a. Salvage value
b. Historical cost
c. Net income per employee
d. Depreciation

3. In finance, the _____s between two currencies specifies how much one currency is worth in terms of the other. It is the value of a foreign natione;s currency in terms of the home natione;s currency. For example an _____ of 102 Japanese yen to the United States dollar means that JPY 102 is worth the same as USD 1.

a. ACCRA Cost of Living Index
b. ACEA agreement
c. Interbank market
d. Exchange rate

4. Economics:

- _____,the desire to own something and the ability to pay for it
- _____ curve,a graphic representation of a _____ schedule
- _____ deposit, the money in checking accounts
- _____ pull theory,the theory that inflation occurs when _____ for goods and services exceeds existing supplies
- _____ schedule,a table that lists the quantity of a good a person will buy it each different price
- _____ side economics,the school of economics at believes government spending and tax cuts open economy by raising _____

a. Demand
b. Variability
c. Production
d. McKesson ' Robbins scandal

5. _____ is money accepted for exchange of goods in an economy. The prevalence of one money over another arises, usually, when a government designates through decrees that the government shall accept only particular notes and coins in payment for taxes. Typically, money of _____ consists of stamped coins and minted paper bills.

Chapter 13. Exchange Rates and Their Determination: A Basic Model

a. Security thread
b. Currency
c. Local currency
d. Totnes pound

6. _____ in economics and business is the result of an exchange and from that trade we assign a numerical monetary value to a good, service or asset. If Alice trades Bob 4 apples for an orange, the _____ of an orange is 4 apples. Inversely, the _____ of an apple is 1/4 oranges.
   a. Price
   b. Price book
   c. Premium pricing
   d. Price war

7. _____ is the price of a commodity such as a good or service in terms of another; ie, the ratio of two prices. A _____ may be expressed in terms of a ratio between any two prices or the ratio between the price of one particular good and a weighted average of all other goods available in the market. A _____ is an opportunity cost.
   a. False economy
   b. False shortage
   c. Food cooperative
   d. Relative price

8. The _____ is where currency trading takes place. It is where banks and other official institutions facilitate the buying and selling of foreign currencies. FX transactions typically involve one party purchasing a quantity of one currency in exchange for paying a quantity of another.
   a. Covered interest arbitrage
   b. Currency swap
   c. Floating currency
   d. Foreign exchange market

9. A _____ is a hypothetical measure of overall prices for some set of goods and services, in a given region during a given interval, normalized relative to some base set. Typically, a _____ is approximated with a price index.

The classical dichotomy is the assumption that there is a relatively clean distinction between overall increases or decreases in prices and underlying, e;reale; economic variables.

   a. Price elasticity of supply
   b. Discretionary spending
   c. Discouraged worker
   d. Price level

10. In economics, _____ is the total demand for final goods and services in the economy (Y) at a given time and price level. It is the amount of goods and services in the economy that will be purchased at all possible price levels. This is the demand for the gross domestic product of a country when inventory levels are static.
    a. Aggregation problem
    b. Aggregate supply
    c. Aggregate expenditure
    d. Aggregate demand

11. _____s is the social science that studies the production, distribution, and consumption of goods and services. The term _____s comes from the Ancient Greek oá¼°κονομῖα from oá¼¶κος (oikos, 'house') + vΐŒμος (nomos, 'custom' or 'law'), hence 'rules of the house(hold)'. Current _____ models developed out of the broader field of political economy in the late 19th century, owing to a desire to use an empirical approach more akin to the physical sciences.
    a. Energy economics
    b. Opportunity cost
    c. Economic
    d. Inflation

12. Formally the _____ is the percentage change in local currency import prices resulting from a one percent change in the exchange rate between the exporting and importing countries. Inevitably the change in the import prices find their way to retail and consumer prices. Inflation pass through occurs when the change in the currency changes prices and therefore inflation.

a. Exchange rate pass-through

b. Optional Protocols to the Convention on the Rights of the Child on the Sale of Children, Child Prostitution and Child Pornography

c. Availability to be borrowed

d. Authorised Deposit-Taking Institutions

13. The term '_____' refers to the concept of collecting information and attempting to spot a pattern in the information. In some fields of study, the term '_____' has more formally-defined meanings.

In project management _____ is a mathematical technique that uses historical results to predict future outcome.

a. Probit model
c. Coefficient of determination

b. Quantile regression
d. Trend analysis

Chapter 14. Money, Interest Rates, and the Exchange Rate

1. In economics, _____ is the total amount of money available in an economy at a particular point in time. There are several ways to define 'money', but standard measures usually include currency in circulation and demand deposits.

    _____ data are recorded and published, usually by the government or the central bank of the country.

    a. Neutrality of money
    b. Velocity of money
    c. Money supply
    d. Veil of money

2. In economics, the _____ is a term relating to the money supply, the amount of money in the economy. The _____ comprises only coins, paper money, and commercial banks' reserves with the central bank. Broader measures of the money supply include the public's bank deposits.

    a. Monetary economy
    b. Chartalism
    c. Quantum economics
    d. Monetary base

3. The most common mechanism used to measure this increase in the money supply is typically called the _____. It calculates the maximum amount of money that an initial deposit can be expanded to with a given reserve ratio - such a factor is called a multiplier.

    The _____, m, is the inverse of the reserve requirement, R:

    $$m = \frac{1}{R}$$

    This formula stems from the fact that the sum of the 'amount loaned out' column above can be expressed mathematically as a geometric series with a common ratio of 1 − R.

    a. Flow to Equity-Approach
    b. Kibbutz volunteers
    c. Fixed-income arbitrage
    d. Money multiplier

4. The _____ is a bank regulation that sets the minimum reserves each bank must hold to customer deposits and notes. It would normally be in the form of fiat currency stored in a bank vault (vault cash), or with a central bank.

    The reserve ratio is sometimes used as a tool in the monetary policy, influencing the country's economy, borrowing, and interest rates.

    a. Fractional-reserve banking
    b. Probability of default
    c. Private money
    d. Reserve requirement

5. Discounting is a financial mechanism in which a debtor obtains the right to delay payments to a creditor, for a defined period of time, in exchange for a charge or fee. Essentially, the party that owes money in the present purchases the right to delay the payment until some future date. The _____, or charge, is simply the difference between the original amount owed in the present and the amount that has to be paid in the future to settle the debt.

    a. Reinsurance
    b. Reliability theory
    c. Certified Risk Manager
    d. Discount

6. The _____ is an interest rate a central bank charges depository institutions that borrow reserves from it.

Chapter 14. Money, Interest Rates, and the Exchange Rate

The term _____ has two meanings:

- the same as interest rate; the term 'discount' does not refer to the meaning of the word, but to the purpose of using the quantity, such as computations of present value, e.g. net present value or discounted cash flow

- the annual effective _____, which is the annual interest divided by the capital including that interest; this rate is lower than the interest rate; it corresponds to using the value after a year as the nominal value, and seeing the initial value as the nominal value minus a discount; it is used for Treasury Bills and similar financial instruments

The annual effective _____ is the annual interest divided by the capital including that interest, which is the interest rate divided by 100% plus the interest rate. It is the annual discount factor to be applied to the future cash flow, to find the discount, subtracted from a future value to find the value one year earlier.

For example, suppose there is a government bond that sells for $95 and pays $100 in a year's time.

a. Perpetuity
c. Johansen test
b. Discount rate
d. Stochastic volatility

7. _____ is the process by which the government, central bank (ii) availability of money, and (iii) cost of money or rate of interest, in order to attain a set of objectives oriented towards the growth and stability of the economy. Monetary theory provides insight into how to craft optimal _____.

_____ is referred to as either being an expansionary policy where an expansionary policy increases the total supply of money in the economy, and a contractionary policy decreases the total money supply.

a. 1921 recession
c. 100-year flood
b. 130-30 fund
d. Monetary policy

8. The _____ is an international organization of central banks which 'fosters international monetary and financial cooperation and serves as a bank for central banks.' It is not accountable to any national government. The BIS carries out its work through subcommittees, the secretariats it hosts, and through its annual General Meeting of all members. It also provides banking services, but only to central banks, or to international organizations like itself.

a. 1921 recession
c. 130-30 fund
b. Bank for International Settlements
d. 100-year flood

9. _____s is the social science that studies the production, distribution, and consumption of goods and services. The term _____s comes from the Ancient Greek οἰκονομία from οἶκος (oikos, 'house') + νόμος (nomos, 'custom' or 'law'), hence 'rules of the house(hold)'. Current _____ models developed out of the broader field of political economy in the late 19th century, owing to a desire to use an empirical approach more akin to the physical sciences.

a. Economic
c. Inflation
b. Energy economics
d. Opportunity cost

10. In economics, the _____ is the term used to refer to the environment in which bonds are bought and sold between a central bank ' its regulated banks. It is not a free market process.

- To intervene in the 'business cycle', a central bank may choose to go into the _____ and buy or sell government bonds, which is known as _____ operations to increase reserves.

a. ACCRA Cost of Living Index
b. Inside money
c. Outside money
d. Open market

11. _____ are the means of implementing monetary policy by which a central bank controls its national money supply by buying and selling government securities, or other financial instruments. Monetary targets, such as interest rates or exchange rates, are used to guide this implementation.

Since most money is now in the form of electronic records, rather than paper records such as banknotes, _____ are conducted simply by electronically increasing or decreasing ('crediting' or 'debiting') the amount of money that a bank has, e.g., in its reserve account at the central bank, in exchange for a bank selling or buying a financial instrument.

a. ACCRA Cost of Living Index
b. ACEA agreement
c. AD-IA Model
d. Open market operations

12. Economics:

- _____, the desire to own something and the ability to pay for it
- _____ curve, a graphic representation of a _____ schedule
- _____ deposit, the money in checking accounts
- _____ pull theory, the theory that inflation occurs when _____ for goods and services exceeds existing supplies
- _____ schedule, a table that lists the quantity of a good a person will buy it each different price
- _____ side economics, the school of economics at believes government spending and tax cuts open economy by raising _____

a. Production
b. Variability
c. McKesson ' Robbins scandal
d. Demand

13. The _____ is the desired holding of money balances in the form of cash or bank deposits.

Money is dominated as store of value by interest bearing assets. However, money is necessary to carry out transactions, or in other words, it provides liquidity.

a. Market neutral
b. Conglomerate merger
c. Borrowing base
d. Demand for money

Chapter 14. Money, Interest Rates, and the Exchange Rate

14. The _____ or gross domestic income (GDI), a basic measure of an economy's economic performance, is the market value of all final goods and services produced within the borders of a nation in a year. _____ can be defined in three ways, all of which are conceptually identical. First, it is equal to the total expenditures for all final goods and services produced within the country in a stipulated period of time (usually a 365-day year.)

  a. Market structure
  b. Monopolistic competition
  c. Countercyclical
  d. Gross Domestic Product

15. _____ in economics and business is the result of an exchange and from that trade we assign a numerical monetary value to a good, service or asset. If Alice trades Bob 4 apples for an orange, the _____ of an orange is 4 apples. Inversely, the _____ of an apple is 1/4 oranges.

  a. Premium pricing
  b. Price book
  c. Price war
  d. Price

16. A _____ is a hypothetical measure of overall prices for some set of goods and services, in a given region during a given interval, normalized relative to some base set. Typically, a _____ is approximated with a price index.

The classical dichotomy is the assumption that there is a relatively clean distinction between overall increases or decreases in prices and underlying, e;reale; economic variables.

  a. Discouraged worker
  b. Discretionary spending
  c. Price elasticity of supply
  d. Price level

17. In economics, _____ is the total demand for final goods and services in the economy (Y) at a given time and price level. It is the amount of goods and services in the economy that will be purchased at all possible price levels. This is the demand for the gross domestic product of a country when inventory levels are static.

  a. Aggregation problem
  b. Aggregate expenditure
  c. Aggregate demand
  d. Aggregate supply

18. In algebra, a _____ is a function depending on n that associates a scalar, det(A), to an n×n square matrix A. The fundamental geometric meaning of a _____ is a scale factor for measure when A is regarded as a linear transformation. _____s are important both in calculus, where they enter the substitution rule for several variables, and in multilinear algebra.

For a fixed nonnegative integer n, there is a unique _____ function for the n×n matrices over any commutative ring R. In particular, this function exists when R is the field of real or complex numbers.

  a. 1921 recession
  b. Determinant
  c. 100-year flood
  d. 130-30 fund

19. _____ is a fee paid on borrowed assets. It is the price paid for the use of borrowed money , or, money earned by deposited funds . Assets that are sometimes lent with _____ include money, shares, consumer goods through hire purchase, major assets such as aircraft, and even entire factories in finance lease arrangements.

  a. Insolvency
  b. Internal debt
  c. Asset protection
  d. Interest

Chapter 14. Money, Interest Rates, and the Exchange Rate

20. An _____ is the price a borrower pays for the use of money they do not own, for instance a small company might borrow from a bank to kick start their business, and the return a lender receives for deferring the use of funds, by lending it to the borrower. _____s are normally expressed as a percentage rate over the period of one year.

_____s targets are also a vital tool of monetary policy and are used to control variables like investment, inflation, and unemployment.

 a. Enterprise value
 b. Arrow-Debreu model
 c. ACCRA Cost of Living Index
 d. Interest rate

21. In economics, the _____ measures the payments that flow between any individual country and all other countries. It is used to summarize all international economic transactions for that country during a specific time period, usually a year. The _____ is determined by the country's exports and imports of goods, services, and financial capital, as well as financial transfers.
 a. Gross world product
 b. Balance of payments
 c. Gross domestic product per barrel
 d. Skyscraper Index

22. A _____ is the transfer of wealth from one party (such as a person or company) to another. A _____ is usually made in exchange for the provision of goods, services or both, or to fulfill a legal obligation.

The simplest and oldest form of _____ is barter, the exchange of one good or service for another.

 a. Soft count
 b. Payment
 c. Going concern
 d. Social gravity

23. In finance, the _____s between two currencies specifies how much one currency is worth in terms of the other. It is the value of a foreign natione;s currency in terms of the home natione;s currency. For example an _____ of 102 Japanese yen to the United States dollar means that JPY 102 is worth the same as USD 1.
 a. Interbank market
 b. Exchange rate
 c. ACEA agreement
 d. ACCRA Cost of Living Index

24. In economics and finance, _____ is the practice of taking advantage of a price differential between two or more markets: striking a combination of matching deals that capitalize upon the imbalance, the profit being the difference between the market prices. When used by academics, an _____ is a transaction that involves no negative cash flow at any probabilistic or temporal state and a positive cash flow in at least one state; in simple terms, a risk-free profit. A person who engages in _____ is called an arbitrageur--such as a bank or brokerage firm.
 a. Arbitrage
 b. Options Price Reporting Authority
 c. Alternext
 d. Electronic trading

25. The _____ is where currency trading takes place. It is where banks and other official institutions facilitate the buying and selling of foreign currencies. FX transactions typically involve one party purchasing a quantity of one currency in exchange for paying a quantity of another.
 a. Floating currency
 b. Currency swap
 c. Covered interest arbitrage
 d. Foreign exchange market

Chapter 15. Price Levels and Exchange Rates in the Long Run

1. _____, 1st Baron Keynes was a renowned economist from Britain whose many ideas on economic and political theories as well as on many governments' monetary policies influenced America. He advocated a government that played an active role in the lives of people regarding business, economy, etc. In this role, the government would use fiscal measures to reduce the consequences of recessions, economic depressions and booms.
   a. Adolf Hitler
   b. Adam Smith
   c. Adolph Fischer
   d. John Maynard Keynes

2. The _____ is an economic law stated as: 'In an efficient market all identical goods must have only one price.' The _____ relates to the outcome of free trade and globalization. It is the theory that some day all areas of the world will make the same amount of money as every other part of the world for equal work/product quality.

   The intuition for this law is that all sellers will flock to the highest prevailing price, and all buyers to the lowest current market price.

   a. Precaria
   b. Loss of use
   c. Leave of absence
   d. Law of one price

3. _____ in economics and business is the result of an exchange and from that trade we assign a numerical monetary value to a good, service or asset. If Alice trades Bob 4 apples for an orange, the _____ of an orange is 4 apples. Inversely, the _____ of an apple is 1/4 oranges.
   a. Premium pricing
   b. Price war
   c. Price book
   d. Price

4. _____ refers to a business or organization attempting to acquire goods or services to accomplish the goals of the enterprise. Though there are several organizations that attempt to set standards in the _____ process, processes can vary greatly between organizations. Typically the word '_____' is not used interchangeably with the word 'procurement', since procurement typically includes Expediting, Supplier Quality, and Traffic and Logistics (T'L) in addition to _____.
   a. 130-30 fund
   b. Free port
   c. 100-year flood
   d. Purchasing

5. _____ is the number of goods/services that can be purchased with a unit of currency. For example, if you had taken one dollar to a store in the 1950s, you would have been able to buy a greater number of items than you would today, indicating that you would have had a greater _____ in the 1950s. Currency can be either a commodity money, like gold or silver, or fiat currency like US dollars.
   a. Purchasing power
   b. Genuine progress indicator
   c. Compliance cost
   d. Human Poverty Index

6. The _____ theory uses the long-term equilibrium exchange rate of two currencies to equalize their purchasing power. Developed by Gustav Cassel in 1920, it is based on the law of one price: the theory states that, in ideally efficient markets, identical goods should have only one price.

   This purchasing power SEM rate equalizes the purchasing power of different currencies in their home countries for a given basket of goods.

   a. Purchasing power parity
   b. Measures of national income and output
   c. Gross national product
   d. Bureau of Labor Statistics

Chapter 15. Price Levels and Exchange Rates in the Long Run

7. A _____ is a hypothetical measure of overall prices for some set of goods and services, in a given region during a given interval, normalized relative to some base set. Typically, a _____ is approximated with a price index.

The classical dichotomy is the assumption that there is a relatively clean distinction between overall increases or decreases in prices and underlying, e;reale; economic variables.

   a. Price elasticity of supply
   b. Discouraged worker
   c. Discretionary spending
   d. Price level

8. In economics, _____ is the total demand for final goods and services in the economy (Y) at a given time and price level. It is the amount of goods and services in the economy that will be purchased at all possible price levels. This is the demand for the gross domestic product of a country when inventory levels are static.
   a. Aggregation problem
   b. Aggregate supply
   c. Aggregate expenditure
   d. Aggregate demand

9. Economics:

   - _____ ,the desire to own something and the ability to pay for it
   - _____ curve,a graphic representation of a _____ schedule
   - _____ deposit, the money in checking accounts
   - _____ pull theory,the theory that inflation occurs when _____ for goods and services exceeds existing supplies
   - _____ schedule,a table that lists the quantity of a good a person will buy it each different price
   - _____ side economics,the school of economics at believes government spending and tax cuts open economy by raising _____

   a. Production
   b. Demand
   c. McKesson ' Robbins scandal
   d. Variability

10. The _____ is published by The Economist as an informal way of measuring the purchasing power parity (PPP) between two currencies and provides a test of the extent to which market exchange rates result in goods costing the same in different countries. It 'seeks to make exchange-rate theory a bit more digestible'.

The index takes its name from the Big Mac, a hamburger sold at McDonald's restaurants.

   a. Cost-weighted activity index
   b. Deindexation
   c. Rank mobility index
   d. Big Mac index

11. _____ is the price of a commodity such as a good or service in terms of another; ie, the ratio of two prices. A _____ may be expressed in terms of a ratio between any two prices or the ratio between the price of one particular good and a weighted average of all other goods available in the market. A _____ is an opportunity cost.
   a. False economy
   b. False shortage
   c. Relative Price
   d. Food cooperative

12. _____s is the social science that studies the production, distribution, and consumption of goods and services. The term _____s comes from the Ancient Greek oá¼°κονομῖα from oá¼¶κος (oikos, 'house') + vÍŒμος (nomos, 'custom' or 'law'), hence 'rules of the house(hold)'. Current _____ models developed out of the broader field of political economy in the late 19th century, owing to a desire to use an empirical approach more akin to the physical sciences.
   a. Economic
   b. Inflation
   c. Opportunity cost
   d. Energy economics

13. _____ is a branch of economics with three main subdisciplines international trade, monetary economics and international finance.

   - International trade studies goods-and-services flows across international boundaries from supply-and-demand factors, economic integration, and policy variables such as tariff rates and trade quotas.
   - International finance studies the flow of capital across international financial markets, and the effects of these movements on exchange rates.
   - International monetary economics and macroeconomics studies money and macro flows across countries.
   - Stanley W. Black (2008.) 'international monetary institutions,' The New Palgrave Dictionary of Economics. 2nd Edition.

   a. ACCRA Cost of Living Index
   b. Index number
   c. Economic depreciation
   d. International Economics

14. _____ is the a method of technical and economic research of the systems for purpose to optimize a parity between system's consumer functions or properties and expenses to achieve those functions or properties.

This methodology for continuous perfection of production, industrial technologies, organizational structures was developed by Juryj Sobolev in 1948 at the 'Perm telephone factory'

   - 1948 Juryj Sobolev - the first success in application of a method analysis at the 'Perm telephone factory'.
   - 1949 - the first application for the invention as result of use of the new method.

Today in economically developed countries practically each enterprise or the company use methodology of the kind of functional-cost analysis as a practice of the quality management, most full satisfying to principles of standards of series ISO 9000.

   - Interest of consumer not in products itself, but the advantage which it will receive from its usage.
   - The consumer aspires to reduce his expenses
   - Functions needed by consumer can be executed in the various ways, and, hence, with various efficiency and expenses. Among possible alternatives of realization of functions exist such in which the parity of quality and the price is the optimal for the consumer.

The goal of _____ is achievement of the highest consumer satisfaction of production at simultaneous decrease in all kinds of industrial expenses Classical _____ has three English synonyms - Value Engineering, Value Management, Value Analysis.

a. Function cost analysis
b. Staple financing
c. Willingness to pay
d. Monopoly wage

15. _____ refers to the additional value of a commodity over the cost of commodities used to produce it from the previous stage of production. An example is the price of gasoline at the pump over the price of the oil in it. In national accounts used in macroeconomics, it refers to the contribution of the factors of production, i.e., land, labor, and capital goods, to raising the value of a product and corresponds to the incomes received by the owners of these factors.
a. Solow residual
b. Hodrick-Prescott filter
c. Value added
d. Full employment

16. _____ , or goods and services tax (GST) is a consumption tax levied on value added. In contrast to sales tax, _____ is neutral with respect to the number of passages that there are between the producer and the final consumer; where sales tax is levied on total value at each stage, the result is a cascade (downstream taxes levied on upstream taxes.) A _____ is an indirect tax, in that the tax is collected from someone who does not bear the entire cost of the tax.
a. Value added tax
b. 130-30 fund
c. 100-year flood
d. 1921 recession

17. To _____ is to impose a financial charge or other levy upon a taxpayer by a state or the functional equivalent of a state.

_____es are also imposed by many subnational entities. _____es consist of direct _____ or indirect _____, and may be paid in money or as its labour equivalent (often but not always unpaid.)

a. 130-30 fund
b. 100-year flood
c. 1921 recession
d. Tax

18. _____ originally was the term for studying production, buying and selling, and their relations with law, custom, and government. _____ originated in moral philosophy. It developed in the 18th century as the study of the economies of states -- polities, hence _____.
a. Geoeconomics
b. Productive and unproductive labour
c. Dirigisme
d. Political Economy

19. The _____ is the desired holding of money balances in the form of cash or bank deposits.

Money is dominated as store of value by interest bearing assets. However, money is necessary to carry out transactions, or in other words, it provides liquidity.

a. Borrowing base
b. Demand for money
c. Conglomerate merger
d. Market neutral

20. The _____ or gross domestic income (GDI), a basic measure of an economy's economic performance, is the market value of all final goods and services produced within the borders of a nation in a year. _____ can be defined in three ways, all of which are conceptually identical. First, it is equal to the total expenditures for all final goods and services produced within the country in a stipulated period of time (usually a 365-day year.)

Chapter 15. Price Levels and Exchange Rates in the Long Run

a. Market structure
c. Gross Domestic Product
b. Countercyclical
d. Monopolistic competition

21. In economics, _____ is the total amount of money available in an economy at a particular point in time. There are several ways to define 'money', but standard measures usually include currency in circulation and demand deposits.

_____ data are recorded and published, usually by the government or the central bank of the country.

a. Veil of money
c. Neutrality of money
b. Velocity of money
d. Money supply

22. In finance, the _____s between two currencies specifies how much one currency is worth in terms of the other. It is the value of a foreign natione;s currency in terms of the home natione;s currency. For example an _____ of 102 Japanese yen to the United States dollar means that JPY 102 is worth the same as USD 1.

a. Interbank market
c. ACEA agreement
b. Exchange rate
d. ACCRA Cost of Living Index

23. The '_____' is approximately the nominal interest rate minus the inflation rate Since the inflation rate over the course of a loan is not known initially, volatility in inflation represents a risk to both the lender and the borrower.

In economics and finance, an individual who lends money for repayment at a later point in time expects to be compensated for the time value of money, or not having the use of that money while it is lent.

a. Reflation
c. Core inflation
b. Cost-push inflation
d. Real interest rate

24. _____ is a fee paid on borrowed assets. It is the price paid for the use of borrowed money, or, money earned by deposited funds. Assets that are sometimes lent with _____ include money, shares, consumer goods through hire purchase, major assets such as aircraft, and even entire factories in finance lease arrangements.

a. Asset protection
c. Insolvency
b. Internal debt
d. Interest

25. An _____ is the price a borrower pays for the use of money they do not own, for instance a small company might borrow from a bank to kick start their business, and the return a lender receives for deferring the use of funds, by lending it to the borrower. _____s are normally expressed as a percentage rate over the period of one year.

_____s targets are also a vital tool of monetary policy and are used to control variables like investment, inflation, and unemployment.

a. ACCRA Cost of Living Index
c. Arrow-Debreu model
b. Enterprise value
d. Interest rate

Chapter 16. Output and the Exchange Rate in the Short Run

1. In economics, _____ is the total demand for final goods and services in the economy (Y) at a given time and price level. It is the amount of goods and services in the economy that will be purchased at all possible price levels. This is the demand for the gross domestic product of a country when inventory levels are static.
   a. Aggregation problem
   b. Aggregate expenditure
   c. Aggregate supply
   d. Aggregate demand

2. _____ is a common concept in economics, and gives rise to derived concepts such as consumer debt. Generally _____ is defined by opposition to production. But the precise definition can vary because different schools of economists define production quite differently.
   a. Federal Reserve Bank Notes
   b. Cash or share options
   c. Foreclosure data providers
   d. Consumption

3. In economics, an _____ is any good or commodity, transported from one country to another country in a legitimate fashion, typically for use in trade. _____ goods or services are provided to foreign consumers by domestic producers. _____ is an important part of international trade.
   a. AD-IA Model
   b. ACEA agreement
   c. ACCRA Cost of Living Index
   d. Export

4. In economics, an _____ is any good (e.g. a commodity) or service brought into one country from another country in a legitimate fashion, typically for use in trade. It is a good that is brought in from another country for sale. _____ goods or services are provided to domestic consumers by foreign producers. An _____ in the receiving country is an export to the sending country.
   a. Import quota
   b. Economic integration
   c. Incoterms
   d. Import

5. Economics:

   - _____, the desire to own something and the ability to pay for it
   - _____ curve, a graphic representation of a _____ schedule
   - _____ deposit, the money in checking accounts
   - _____ pull theory, the theory that inflation occurs when _____ for goods and services exceeds existing supplies
   - _____ schedule, a table that lists the quantity of a good a person will buy it each different price
   - _____ side economics, the school of economics at believes government spending and tax cuts open economy by raising _____

   a. Demand
   b. Production
   c. McKesson ' Robbins scandal
   d. Variability

6. The _____ or gross domestic income (GDI), a basic measure of an economy's economic performance, is the market value of all final goods and services produced within the borders of a nation in a year. _____ can be defined in three ways, all of which are conceptually identical. First, it is equal to the total expenditures for all final goods and services produced within the country in a stipulated period of time (usually a 365-day year.)
   a. Monopolistic competition
   b. Gross domestic product
   c. Market structure
   d. Countercyclical

Chapter 16. Output and the Exchange Rate in the Short Run

7. _____ is a fee paid on borrowed assets. It is the price paid for the use of borrowed money, or, money earned by deposited funds. Assets that are sometimes lent with _____ include money, shares, consumer goods through hire purchase, major assets such as aircraft, and even entire factories in finance lease arrangements.
   a. Asset protection
   b. Insolvency
   c. Interest
   d. Internal debt

8. An _____ is the price a borrower pays for the use of money they do not own, for instance a small company might borrow from a bank to kick start their business, and the return a lender receives for deferring the use of funds, by lending it to the borrower. _____s are normally expressed as a percentage rate over the period of one year.

   _____s targets are also a vital tool of monetary policy and are used to control variables like investment, inflation, and unemployment.

   a. Enterprise value
   b. ACCRA Cost of Living Index
   c. Interest rate
   d. Arrow-Debreu model

9. The _____ is an economic term, referring to an increase in spending that accompanies an increase or perceived increase in wealth.

   The effect would cause changes in the amounts and composition of consumer consumption caused by changes in consumer wealth. People should spend more when one of two things is true: when people actually are richer (by objective measurement, for example, a bonus or a pay raise at work, which would be an income effect), or when people perceive themselves to be 'richer' (for example, the assessed value of their home increases, or a stock they own has gone up in price recently.)

   a. Wealth effect
   b. Wealth condensation
   c. 100-year flood
   d. 130-30 fund

10. In finance, the _____s between two currencies specifies how much one currency is worth in terms of the other. It is the value of a foreign natione;s currency in terms of the home natione;s currency. For example an _____ of 102 Japanese yen to the United States dollar means that JPY 102 is worth the same as USD 1.
    a. ACEA agreement
    b. ACCRA Cost of Living Index
    c. Interbank market
    d. Exchange rate

11. _____ or government expenditure is classified by economists into three main types. Government purchases of goods and services for current use are classed as government consumption. Government purchases of goods and services intended to create future benefits, such as infrastructure investment or research spending, are classed as government investment.
    a. 100-year flood
    b. 130-30 fund
    c. 1921 recession
    d. Government spending

12. _____ in economics and business is the result of an exchange and from that trade we assign a numerical monetary value to a good, service or asset. If Alice trades Bob 4 apples for an orange, the _____ of an orange is 4 apples. Inversely, the _____ of an apple is 1/4 oranges.

Chapter 16. Output and the Exchange Rate in the Short Run

a. Price book
b. Price war
c. Premium pricing
d. Price

13. A _____ is a hypothetical measure of overall prices for some set of goods and services, in a given region during a given interval, normalized relative to some base set. Typically, a _____ is approximated with a price index.

The classical dichotomy is the assumption that there is a relatively clean distinction between overall increases or decreases in prices and underlying, e;reale; economic variables.

a. Price elasticity of supply
b. Price level
c. Discouraged worker
d. Discretionary spending

14. In economics, _____ is the total supply of goods and services produced by a national economy during a specific time period. It is the total amount of goods and services in the economy available at all possible price levels.
a. Aggregation problem
b. Aggregate expenditure
c. Aggregate demand
d. Aggregate supply

15. In algebra, a _____ is a function depending on n that associates a scalar, det(A), to an n×n square matrix A. The fundamental geometric meaning of a _____ is a scale factor for measure when A is regarded as a linear transformation. _____s are important both in calculus, where they enter the substitution rule for several variables, and in multilinear algebra.

For a fixed nonnegative integer n, there is a unique _____ function for the n×n matrices over any commutative ring R. In particular, this function exists when R is the field of real or complex numbers.

a. 130-30 fund
b. 100-year flood
c. Determinant
d. 1921 recession

16. In economics, _____ are the resources employed to produce goods and services. They facilitate production but do not become part of the product (as with raw materials) or significantly transformed by the production process (as with fuel used to power machinery.) To 19th century economists, the _____ were land (natural resources, gifts from nature), labor (the ability to work), and capital goods (human-made tools and equipment.)
a. Product Pipeline
b. Long-run
c. Hicks-neutral technical change
d. Factors of production

17. In microeconomics, _____ is quite simply the conversion of inputs into outputs. It is an economic process that uses resources to create a good or service that is suitable for exchange. This can include manufacturing, storing, shipping, and packaging.
a. MET
b. Red Guards
c. Solved
d. Production

18. _____, or a _____ is the concept of a resulting effect (cf. cause and effect, arising from another action. In general terms, it is used to indicate that all human actions, particularly crime and sin, have profound effects.
a. Variability
b. Solved
c. Consequence
d. Rule

Chapter 16. Output and the Exchange Rate in the Short Run

19. In economics, the _____ is one of the two primary components of the balance of payments, the other being the capital account. It is the sum of the balance of trade (exports minus imports of goods and services), net factor income (such as interest and dividends) and net transfer payments (such as foreign aid.)

$$\text{Current account} = \text{Balance of trade}$$
$$+ \text{Net factor income from abroad}$$
$$+ \text{Net unilateral transfers from abroad}$$

The _____ balance is one of two major metrics of the nature of a country's foreign trade (the other being the net capital outflow.)

  a. Gross private domestic investment
  b. Current account
  c. Compensation of employees
  d. National Income and Product Accounts

20. In economics, the _____ of demand measures the responsiveness of the demand of a good to the change in the income of the people demanding the good. It is calculated as the ratio of the percent change in demand to the percent change in income. For example, if, in response to a 10% increase in income, the demand of a good increased by 20%, the _____ of demand would be 20%/10% = 2.
  a. ACEA agreement
  b. ACCRA Cost of Living Index
  c. AD-IA Model
  d. Income elasticity

21. In economics, the _____ measures the responsiveness of the demand of a good to the change in the income of the people demanding the good. It is calculated as the ratio of the percent change in demand to the percent change in income. For example, if, in response to a 10% increase in income, the demand of a good increased by 20%, the _____ would be 20%/10% = 2.
  a. Expenditure minimization problem
  b. Elasticity of substitution
  c. Indifference map
  d. Income elasticity of demand

22. In economics, _____ is the ratio of the percent change in one variable to the percent change in another variable. It is a tool for measuring the responsiveness of a function to changes in parameters in a relative way. Commonly analyzed are _____ of substitution, price and wealth.
  a. ACEA agreement
  b. ACCRA Cost of Living Index
  c. Elasticity of demand
  d. Elasticity

23. Price _____ is defined as the measure of responsiveness in the quantity demanded for a commodity as a result of change in price of the same commodity. It is a measure of how consumers react to a change in price. In other words, it is percentage change in quantity demanded by the percentage change in price of the same commodity.
  a. Elasticity
  b. ACCRA Cost of Living Index
  c. ACEA agreement
  d. Elasticity of demand

24. _____ is defined as the measure of responsiveness in the quantity demanded for a commodity as a result of change in price of the same commodity. It is a measure of how consumers react to a change in price. In other words, it is percentage change in quantity demanded as per the percentage change in price of the same commodity.

Chapter 16. Output and the Exchange Rate in the Short Run

a. 130-30 fund
c. 100-year flood
b. Price elasticity of demand
d. 1921 recession

25. _____s is the social science that studies the production, distribution, and consumption of goods and services. The term _____s comes from the Ancient Greek οἰκονομία from οἶκος (oikos, 'house') + νόμος (nomos, 'custom' or 'law'), hence 'rules of the house(hold)'. Current _____ models developed out of the broader field of political economy in the late 19th century, owing to a desire to use an empirical approach more akin to the physical sciences.
 a. Energy economics
 c. Inflation
 b. Economic
 d. Opportunity cost

26. _____ or human capital flight is a large emigration of individuals with technical skills or knowledge, normally due to conflict, lack of opportunity, political instability, or health risks. _____ is usually regarded as an economic cost, since emigrants usually take with them the fraction of value of their training sponsored by the government. It is a parallel of capital flight which refers to the same movement of financial capital.
 a. 100-year flood
 c. Brain drain
 b. 130-30 fund
 d. 1921 recession

27. A _____ or a flexible exchange rate is a type of exchange rate regime wherein a currency's value is allowed to fluctuate according to the foreign exchange market. A currency that uses a _____ is known as a floating currency. The opposite of a _____ is a fixed exchange rate.
 a. Trade Weighted US dollar Index
 c. Floating currency
 b. Foreign exchange market
 d. Floating exchange rate

28. An _____ is an economy in which people, including businesses, can trade in goods and services with other people and businesses in the international community at large. This contrasts with a closed economy in which international trade cannot take place.

The act of selling goods or services to a foreign country is called exporting.

 a. Attention work
 c. Open economy
 b. Indicative planning
 d. Information economy

29. A _____ is an object whose consumption increases the utility of the consumer, for which the quantity demanded exceeds the quantity supplied at zero price. _____s are usually modeled as having diminishing marginal utility. The first individual purchase has high utility; the second has less.
 a. Composite good
 c. Merit good
 b. Pie method
 d. Good

30. The term '_____' refers to the concept of collecting information and attempting to spot a pattern in the information. In some fields of study, the term '_____' has more formally-defined meanings.

In project management _____ is a mathematical technique that uses historical results to predict future outcome.

a. Trend analysis
b. Coefficient of determination
c. Quantile regression
d. Probit model

Chapter 17. Macroeconomic Policy and Floating Exchange Rates

1. _____s is the social science that studies the production, distribution, and consumption of goods and services. The term _____s comes from the Ancient Greek οἰκονομία from οἶκος (oikos, 'house') + νόμος (nomos, 'custom' or 'law'), hence 'rules of the house(hold)'. Current _____ models developed out of the broader field of political economy in the late 19th century, owing to a desire to use an empirical approach more akin to the physical sciences.

   a. Opportunity cost
   b. Economic
   c. Energy economics
   d. Inflation

2. _____ was an American economist, statistician and public intellectual, and a recipient of the Nobel Memorial Prize in Economic Sciences. He is best known among scholars for his theoretical and empirical research, especially consumption analysis, monetary history and theory, and for his demonstration of the complexity of stabilization policy. A global public followed his restatement of a political philosophy that insisted on minimizing the role of government in favor of the private sector.

   a. Milton Friedman
   b. Adam Smith
   c. Adolph Fischer
   d. Adolf Hitler

3. The _____ is an international organization that oversees the global financial system by following the macroeconomic policies of its member countries, in particular those with an impact on exchange rates and the balance of payments. It is an organization formed to stabilize international exchange rates and facilitate development. It also offers financial and technical assistance to its members, making it an international lender of last resort.

   a. ACEA agreement
   b. ACCRA Cost of Living Index
   c. Office of Thrift Supervision
   d. International Monetary Fund

4. The term _____ refers to government debt, expenditures and revenues, or to finance (particularly financial revenue) in general.

   - _____ deficit is the budget deficit of federal or local government
   - _____ policy is the discretionary spending of governments. Contrasts with monetary policy.
   - _____ year and _____ quarter are reporting periods for firms and other agencies.

   a. Procter ' Gamble
   b. Fiscal
   c. Bucket shop
   d. Drawdown

5. In economics, _____ is the use of government spending and revenue collection to influence the economy.

   _____ can be contrasted with the other main type of economic policy, monetary policy, which attempts to stabilize the economy by controlling interest rates and the supply of money. The two main instruments of _____ are government spending and taxation.

   a. 100-year flood
   b. Sustainable investment rule
   c. Fiscalism
   d. Fiscal policy

6. _____ or government expenditure is classified by economists into three main types. Government purchases of goods and services for current use are classed as government consumption. Government purchases of goods and services intended to create future benefits, such as infrastructure investment or research spending, are classed as government investment.

Chapter 17. Macroeconomic Policy and Floating Exchange Rates

a. 100-year flood
b. 130-30 fund
c. 1921 recession
d. Government spending

7. _____ in economics is a state in which a country maintains full employment and price level stability. It is a function of a country's total output,

$$II = C(Yf - T) + I + G + CA(E \times P^*/P, Yf-T; Yf^* - T^*)$$

_____ = Consumption [determined by disposable income] + Investment + Government Spending + Current Account (determined by the real exchange rate, disposable income of home country and disposable income of the foreign country.)

External balance signifies a condition in which the country's current account, its exports minus imports, is neither too far in surplus nor in deficit.

a. Energy intensity
b. Autonomous consumption
c. Uneconomic growth
d. Internal balance

8. _____ is the process by which the government, central bank (ii) availability of money, and (iii) cost of money or rate of interest, in order to attain a set of objectives oriented towards the growth and stability of the economy. Monetary theory provides insight into how to craft optimal _____.

_____ is referred to as either being an expansionary policy where an expansionary policy increases the total supply of money in the economy, and a contractionary policy decreases the total money supply.

a. 130-30 fund
b. 100-year flood
c. 1921 recession
d. Monetary policy

9. In economics, _____ is the total demand for final goods and services in the economy (Y) at a given time and price level. It is the amount of goods and services in the economy that will be purchased at all possible price levels. This is the demand for the gross domestic product of a country when inventory levels are static.

a. Aggregate expenditure
b. Aggregate supply
c. Aggregation problem
d. Aggregate demand

10. Economics:

- _____, the desire to own something and the ability to pay for it
- _____ curve, a graphic representation of a _____ schedule
- _____ deposit, the money in checking accounts
- _____ pull theory, the theory that inflation occurs when _____ for goods and services exceeds existing supplies
- _____ schedule, a table that lists the quantity of a good a person will buy it each different price
- _____ side economics, the school of economics at believes government spending and tax cuts open economy by raising _____

Chapter 17. Macroeconomic Policy and Floating Exchange Rates

a. McKesson ' Robbins scandal
c. Variability
b. Production
d. Demand

11. _____ is a common concept in economics, and gives rise to derived concepts such as consumer debt. Generally _____ is defined by opposition to production. But the precise definition can vary because different schools of economists define production quite differently.
   a. Cash or share options
   c. Federal Reserve Bank Notes
   b. Foreclosure data providers
   d. Consumption

12. In finance, the _____s between two currencies specifies how much one currency is worth in terms of the other. It is the value of a foreign natione;s currency in terms of the home natione;s currency. For example an _____ of 102 Japanese yen to the United States dollar means that JPY 102 is worth the same as USD 1.
   a. ACEA agreement
   c. Interbank market
   b. Exchange rate
   d. ACCRA Cost of Living Index

13. The _____ or gross domestic income (GDI), a basic measure of an economy's economic performance, is the market value of all final goods and services produced within the borders of a nation in a year. _____ can be defined in three ways, all of which are conceptually identical. First, it is equal to the total expenditures for all final goods and services produced within the country in a stipulated period of time (usually a 365-day year.)
   a. Monopolistic competition
   c. Gross Domestic Product
   b. Countercyclical
   d. Market structure

14. _____ is a fee paid on borrowed assets. It is the price paid for the use of borrowed money , or, money earned by deposited funds . Assets that are sometimes lent with _____ include money, shares, consumer goods through hire purchase, major assets such as aircraft, and even entire factories in finance lease arrangements.
   a. Interest
   c. Internal debt
   b. Insolvency
   d. Asset protection

15. An _____ is the price a borrower pays for the use of money they do not own, for instance a small company might borrow from a bank to kick start their business, and the return a lender receives for deferring the use of funds, by lending it to the borrower. _____s are normally expressed as a percentage rate over the period of one year.

_____s targets are also a vital tool of monetary policy and are used to control variables like investment, inflation, and unemployment.

   a. Enterprise value
   c. Interest rate
   b. Arrow-Debreu model
   d. ACCRA Cost of Living Index

16. _____ in economics and business is the result of an exchange and from that trade we assign a numerical monetary value to a good, service or asset. If Alice trades Bob 4 apples for an orange, the _____ of an orange is 4 apples. Inversely, the _____ of an apple is 1/4 oranges.
   a. Price war
   c. Premium pricing
   b. Price
   d. Price book

17. A _____ is a hypothetical measure of overall prices for some set of goods and services, in a given region during a given interval, normalized relative to some base set. Typically, a _____ is approximated with a price index.

The classical dichotomy is the assumption that there is a relatively clean distinction between overall increases or decreases in prices and underlying, e;reale; economic variables.

a. Price elasticity of supply
b. Discretionary spending
c. Discouraged worker
d. Price level

18. In economics, the _____ measures the payments that flow between any individual country and all other countries. It is used to summarize all international economic transactions for that country during a specific time period, usually a year. The _____ is determined by the country's exports and imports of goods, services, and financial capital, as well as financial transfers.

a. Gross world product
b. Balance of payments
c. Skyscraper Index
d. Gross domestic product per barrel

19. In economics, the _____ is one of the two primary components of the balance of payments, the other being the capital account. It is the sum of the balance of trade (exports minus imports of goods and services), net factor income (such as interest and dividends) and net transfer payments (such as foreign aid.)

$$\text{Current account} = \text{Balance of trade} \\ + \text{Net factor income from abroad} \\ + \text{Net unilateral transfers from abroad}$$

The _____ balance is one of two major metrics of the nature of a country's foreign trade (the other being the net capital outflow.)

a. Current account
b. National Income and Product Accounts
c. Compensation of employees
d. Gross private domestic investment

20. A _____, sometimes called a pegged exchange rate, is a type of exchange rate regime wherein a currency's value is matched to the value of another single currency or to a basket of other currencies such as gold.

A _____ is usually used to stabilize the value of a currency, vis-a-vis the currency it is pegged to. This facilitates trade and investments between the two countries, and is especially useful for small economies where external trade forms a large part of their GDP.

a. Monetary economics
b. Law of supply
c. Leading indicators
d. Fixed exchange rate

21. A _____ or a flexible exchange rate is a type of exchange rate regime wherein a currency's value is allowed to fluctuate according to the foreign exchange market. A currency that uses a _____ is known as a floating currency. The opposite of a _____ is a fixed exchange rate.

a. Trade Weighted US dollar Index
b. Floating exchange rate
c. Foreign exchange market
d. Floating currency

Chapter 17. Macroeconomic Policy and Floating Exchange Rates

22. In economics, the _____ market is a hypothetical market that brings savers and borrowers together, also bringing together the money available in commercial banks and lending institutions available for firms and households to finance expenditures, either investments or consumption. Savers supply the _____; for instance, buying bonds will transfer their money to the institution issuing the bond, which can be a firm or government. In return, borrowers demand _____; when an institution sells a bond, it is demanding _____.
   - a. Spatial inequality
   - b. Reservation wage
   - c. Buffer stock scheme
   - d. Loanable funds

23. A _____ is the transfer of wealth from one party (such as a person or company) to another. A _____ is usually made in exchange for the provision of goods, services or both, or to fulfill a legal obligation.

The simplest and oldest form of _____ is barter, the exchange of one good or service for another.

   - a. Soft count
   - b. Payment
   - c. Going concern
   - d. Social gravity

24. _____ is monetary policy that seeks to increase the size of the money supply. In most nations, monetary policy is controlled by either a central bank or a finance ministry

Neoclassical and Keynesian economics significantly differ on the effects and effectiveness of monetary policy on influencing the real economy; there is no clear consensus on how monetary policy affects real economic variables (aggregate output or income, employment.) Both economic schools accept that monetary policy affects monetary variables (price levels, interest rates.)

   - a. ACEA agreement
   - b. ACCRA Cost of Living Index
   - c. AD-IA Model
   - d. Expansionary monetary policy

25. _____ is monetary policy that seeks to reduce the size of the money supply. They are fiscal policies, like lower spending and higher taxes, that reduce economic growth. In most nations, monetary policy is controlled by either a central bank or a finance ministry.
   - a. Money creation
   - b. Shadow Open Market Committee
   - c. Monetary policy of Sweden
   - d. Contractionary monetary policy

26. The _____ hypothesis is a concept from macroeconomics that contends that there is a strong link between a national economy's current account balance and its government budget balance. As an example, it is hypothesized that a large budget deficit leads to a large current account deficit. The theory goes as follows:

$Y = C + I + G + NX$

where Y represents National Income or GDP, C is consumption, I is investment, G is government spending and NX stands for net exports.

   - a. Public-private partnership
   - b. Power of the purse
   - c. 100-year flood
   - d. Twin deficits

27. _____ are banks' holdings of deposits in accounts with their central bank (for instance the European Central Bank or the Federal Reserve, in the latter case including federal funds), plus currency that is physically held in bank vaults (vault cash.) The central banks of some nations set minimum reserve requirements. Even when no requirements are set, banks commonly wish to hold some reserves, called desired reserves, against unexpected events.

a. Structuring
b. Sweep account
c. Bank reserves
d. Bilateral netting

28. In economics, the _____ is a term relating to the money supply, the amount of money in the economy. The _____ comprises only coins, paper money, and commercial banks' reserves with the central bank. Broader measures of the money supply include the public's bank deposits.

a. Chartalism
b. Quantum economics
c. Monetary economy
d. Monetary base

29. In economics, _____ is the total amount of money available in an economy at a particular point in time. There are several ways to define 'money', but standard measures usually include currency in circulation and demand deposits.

_____ data are recorded and published, usually by the government or the central bank of the country.

a. Veil of money
b. Velocity of money
c. Neutrality of money
d. Money supply

Chapter 18. Fixed Exchange Rates and Currency Unions

1. _____ or human capital flight is a large emigration of individuals with technical skills or knowledge, normally due to conflict, lack of opportunity, political instability, or health risks. _____ is usually regarded as an economic cost, since emigrants usually take with them the fraction of value of their training sponsored by the government. It is a parallel of capital flight which refers to the same movement of financial capital.

   a. Brain drain
   b. 130-30 fund
   c. 1921 recession
   d. 100-year flood

2. _____ is money accepted for exchange of goods in an economy. The prevalence of one money over another arises, usually, when a government designates through decrees that the government shall accept only particular notes and coins in payment for taxes. Typically, money of _____ consists of stamped coins and minted paper bills.

   a. Security thread
   b. Currency
   c. Local currency
   d. Totnes pound

3. A _____ is a monetary authority which is required to maintain a fixed exchange rate with a foreign currency. This policy objective requires the conventional objectives of a central bank to be subordinated to the exchange rate target.

   The main qualities of an orthodox _____ are:

   - A _____'s foreign currency reserves must be sufficient to ensure that all holders of its notes and coins (and all banks creditor of a Reserve Account at the _____) can convert them into the reserve currency (usually 110-115% of the monetary base M0.)
   - A _____ maintains absolute, unlimited convertibility between its notes and coins and the currency against which they are pegged (the anchor currency), at a fixed rate of exchange, with no restrictions on current-account or capital-account transactions.
   - A _____ only earns profit from interests on foreign reserves (less the expense of note-issuing), and does not engage in forward-exchange transactions. These foreign reserves exist (1) because local notes have been issued in exchange, or (2) because commercial banks must by regulation deposit a minimum reserve at the _____. (1) generates a seignorage revenue. (2) is the revenue on minimum reserves (revenue of investment activities less cost of minimum reserves remuneration)
   - A _____ has no discretionary powers to effect monetary policy and does not lend to the government. Governments cannot print money, and can only tax or borrow to meet their spending commitments.
   - A _____ does not act as a lender of last resort to commercial banks, and does not regulate reserve requirements.
   - A _____ does not attempt to manipulate interest rates by establishing a discount rate like a central bank. The peg with the foreign currency tends to keep interest rates and inflation very closely aligned to those in the country against whose currency the peg is fixed.

   The _____ in question will no longer issue fiat money but instead will only issue one unit of local currency for each unit (or decided amount) of foreign currency it has in its vault (often a hard currency such as the U.S. dollar or the euro.) The surplus on the balance of payments of that country is reflected by higher deposits local banks hold at the central bank as well as (initially) higher deposits of the (net) exporting firms at their local banks.

   a. Currency board
   b. Reserve currency
   c. Currency competition
   d. Petrodollar

Chapter 18. Fixed Exchange Rates and Currency Unions

4. In economics, _____ is the total demand for final goods and services in the economy (Y) at a given time and price level. It is the amount of goods and services in the economy that will be purchased at all possible price levels. This is the demand for the gross domestic product of a country when inventory levels are static.
   a. Aggregation problem
   b. Aggregate expenditure
   c. Aggregate supply
   d. Aggregate demand

5. Economics:

   - _____, the desire to own something and the ability to pay for it
   - _____ curve, a graphic representation of a _____ schedule
   - _____ deposit, the money in checking accounts
   - _____ pull theory, the theory that inflation occurs when _____ for goods and services exceeds existing supplies
   - _____ schedule, a table that lists the quantity of a good a person will buy it each different price
   - _____ side economics, the school of economics at believes government spending and tax cuts open economy by raising _____

   a. Variability
   b. Production
   c. McKesson ' Robbins scandal
   d. Demand

6. In finance, the _____s between two currencies specifies how much one currency is worth in terms of the other. It is the value of a foreign natione;s currency in terms of the home natione;s currency. For example an _____ of 102 Japanese yen to the United States dollar means that JPY 102 is worth the same as USD 1.
   a. ACCRA Cost of Living Index
   b. ACEA agreement
   c. Interbank market
   d. Exchange rate

7. _____ is monetary policy that seeks to reduce the size of the money supply. They are fiscal policies, like lower spending and higher taxes, that reduce economic growth. In most nations, monetary policy is controlled by either a central bank or a finance ministry.
   a. Money creation
   b. Shadow Open Market Committee
   c. Monetary policy of Sweden
   d. Contractionary monetary policy

8. The _____ is where currency trading takes place. It is where banks and other official institutions facilitate the buying and selling of foreign currencies. FX transactions typically involve one party purchasing a quantity of one currency in exchange for paying a quantity of another.
   a. Covered interest arbitrage
   b. Currency swap
   c. Floating currency
   d. Foreign exchange market

9. The _____ or gross domestic income (GDI), a basic measure of an economy's economic performance, is the market value of all final goods and services produced within the borders of a nation in a year. _____ can be defined in three ways, all of which are conceptually identical. First, it is equal to the total expenditures for all final goods and services produced within the country in a stipulated period of time (usually a 365-day year.)
   a. Countercyclical
   b. Market structure
   c. Gross Domestic Product
   d. Monopolistic competition

Chapter 18. Fixed Exchange Rates and Currency Unions

10. _____ in economics and business is the result of an exchange and from that trade we assign a numerical monetary value to a good, service or asset. If Alice trades Bob 4 apples for an orange, the _____ of an orange is 4 apples. Inversely, the _____ of an apple is 1/4 oranges.

   a. Price war
   b. Price book
   c. Premium pricing
   d. Price

11. A _____ is a hypothetical measure of overall prices for some set of goods and services, in a given region during a given interval, normalized relative to some base set. Typically, a _____ is approximated with a price index.

The classical dichotomy is the assumption that there is a relatively clean distinction between overall increases or decreases in prices and underlying, e;reale; economic variables.

   a. Discretionary spending
   b. Price elasticity of supply
   c. Discouraged worker
   d. Price level

12. _____, in economics, occurs when assets and/or money rapidly flow out of a country, due to an economic event that disturbs investors and causes them to lower their valuation of the assets in that country, or otherwise to lose confidence in its economic strength. This leads to a disappearance of wealth and is usually accompanied by a sharp drop in the exchange rate of the affected country (depreciation in a variable exchange rate regime, or a forced devaluation in a fixed exchange rate regime.)

This fall is particularly damaging when the capital belongs to the people of the affected country, because not only are the citizens now burdened by the loss of faith in the economy and devaluation of their currency, but probably also their assets have lost much of their nominal value.

   a. Firm-specific infrastructure
   b. Capital formation
   c. Capital flight
   d. Liquid capital

13. A _____, sometimes called a pegged exchange rate, is a type of exchange rate regime wherein a currency's value is matched to the value of another single currency or to a basket of other currencies such as gold.

A _____ is usually used to stabilize the value of a currency, vis-a-vis the currency it is pegged to. This facilitates trade and investments between the two countries, and is especially useful for small economies where external trade forms a large part of their GDP.

   a. Leading indicators
   b. Monetary economics
   c. Law of supply
   d. Fixed exchange rate

14. _____ is the process by which the government, central bank (ii) availability of money, and (iii) cost of money or rate of interest, in order to attain a set of objectives oriented towards the growth and stability of the economy. Monetary theory provides insight into how to craft optimal _____.

_____ is referred to as either being an expansionary policy where an expansionary policy increases the total supply of money in the economy, and a contractionary policy decreases the total money supply.

Chapter 18. Fixed Exchange Rates and Currency Unions

a. Monetary policy
b. 100-year flood
c. 1921 recession
d. 130-30 fund

15. _____ is the a method of technical and economic research of the systems for purpose to optimize a parity between system's consumer functions or properties and expenses to achieve those functions or properties.

This methodology for continuous perfection of production, industrial technologies, organizational structures was developed by Juryj Sobolev in 1948 at the 'Perm telephone factory'

- 1948 Juryj Sobolev - the first success in application of a method analysis at the 'Perm telephone factory' .
- 1949 - the first application for the invention as result of use of the new method.

Today in economically developed countries practically each enterprise or the company use methodology of the kind of functional-cost analysis as a practice of the quality management, most full satisfying to principles of standards of series ISO 9000.

- Interest of consumer not in products itself, but the advantage which it will receive from its usage.
- The consumer aspires to reduce his expenses
- Functions needed by consumer can be executed in the various ways, and, hence, with various efficiency and expenses. Among possible alternatives of realization of functions exist such in which the parity of quality and the price is the optimal for the consumer.

The goal of _____ is achievement of the highest consumer satisfaction of production at simultaneous decrease in all kinds of industrial expenses Classical _____ has three English synonyms - Value Engineering, Value Management, Value Analysis.

a. Willingness to pay
b. Staple financing
c. Monopoly wage
d. Function cost analysis

16. _____ is a fee paid on borrowed assets. It is the price paid for the use of borrowed money , or, money earned by deposited funds . Assets that are sometimes lent with _____ include money, shares, consumer goods through hire purchase, major assets such as aircraft, and even entire factories in finance lease arrangements.

a. Asset protection
b. Insolvency
c. Internal debt
d. Interest

17. An _____ is the price a borrower pays for the use of money they do not own, for instance a small company might borrow from a bank to kick start their business, and the return a lender receives for deferring the use of funds, by lending it to the borrower. _____s are normally expressed as a percentage rate over the period of one year.

_____s targets are also a vital tool of monetary policy and are used to control variables like investment, inflation, and unemployment.

a. ACCRA Cost of Living Index
b. Enterprise value
c. Arrow-Debreu model
d. Interest rate

Chapter 18. Fixed Exchange Rates and Currency Unions

18. In economics, the _____ measures the payments that flow between any individual country and all other countries. It is used to summarize all international economic transactions for that country during a specific time period, usually a year. The _____ is determined by the country's exports and imports of goods, services, and financial capital, as well as financial transfers.

   a. Skyscraper Index
   b. Gross domestic product per barrel
   c. Gross world product
   d. Balance of payments

19. The term _____ refers to government debt, expenditures and revenues, or to finance (particularly financial revenue) in general.

   - _____ deficit is the budget deficit of federal or local government
   - _____ policy is the discretionary spending of governments. Contrasts with monetary policy.
   - _____ year and _____ quarter are reporting periods for firms and other agencies.

   a. Fiscal
   b. Drawdown
   c. Procter ' Gamble
   d. Bucket shop

20. In economics, _____ is the use of government spending and revenue collection to influence the economy.

   _____ can be contrasted with the other main type of economic policy, monetary policy, which attempts to stabilize the economy by controlling interest rates and the supply of money. The two main instruments of _____ are government spending and taxation.

   a. Fiscalism
   b. 100-year flood
   c. Sustainable investment rule
   d. Fiscal policy

21. In economics, the _____ market is a hypothetical market that brings savers and borrowers together, also bringing together the money available in commercial banks and lending institutions available for firms and households to finance expenditures, either investments or consumption. Savers supply the _____; for instance, buying bonds will transfer their money to the institution issuing the bond, which can be a firm or government. In return, borrowers demand _____; when an institution sells a bond, it is demanding _____.

   a. Buffer stock scheme
   b. Loanable funds
   c. Spatial inequality
   d. Reservation wage

22. A _____ is the transfer of wealth from one party (such as a person or company) to another. A _____ is usually made in exchange for the provision of goods, services or both, or to fulfill a legal obligation.

   The simplest and oldest form of _____ is barter, the exchange of one good or service for another.

   a. Payment
   b. Soft count
   c. Going concern
   d. Social gravity

23. _____ is monetary policy that seeks to increase the size of the money supply. In most nations, monetary policy is controlled by either a central bank or a finance ministry

Chapter 18. Fixed Exchange Rates and Currency Unions

Neoclassical and Keynesian economics significantly differ on the effects and effectiveness of monetary policy on influencing the real economy; there is no clear consensus on how monetary policy affects real economic variables (aggregate output or income, employment.) Both economic schools accept that monetary policy affects monetary variables (price levels, interest rates.)

a. ACEA agreement
b. AD-IA Model
c. ACCRA Cost of Living Index
d. Expansionary monetary policy

24. In economics, _____ is the total amount of money available in an economy at a particular point in time. There are several ways to define 'money', but standard measures usually include currency in circulation and demand deposits.

_____ data are recorded and published, usually by the government or the central bank of the country.

a. Neutrality of money
b. Veil of money
c. Velocity of money
d. Money supply

25. In economics, the _____ is the term used to refer to the environment in which bonds are bought and sold between a central bank ' its regulated banks. It is not a free market process.

- To intervene in the 'business cycle', a central bank may choose to go into the _____ and buy or sell government bonds, which is known as _____ operations to increase reserves.

a. ACCRA Cost of Living Index
b. Outside money
c. Inside money
d. Open market

26. _____ are the means of implementing monetary policy by which a central bank controls its national money supply by buying and selling government securities, or other financial instruments. Monetary targets, such as interest rates or exchange rates, are used to guide this implementation.

Since most money is now in the form of electronic records, rather than paper records such as banknotes, _____ are conducted simply by electronically increasing or decreasing ('crediting' or 'debiting') the amount of money that a bank has, e.g., in its reserve account at the central bank, in exchange for a bank selling or buying a financial instrument.

a. ACEA agreement
b. ACCRA Cost of Living Index
c. AD-IA Model
d. Open market operations

27. _____s is the social science that studies the production, distribution, and consumption of goods and services. The term _____s comes from the Ancient Greek oá¼°κονομῖα from oá¼¶κος (oikos, 'house') + vῐ´Œμος (nomos, 'custom' or 'law'), hence 'rules of the house(hold)'. Current _____ models developed out of the broader field of political economy in the late 19th century, owing to a desire to use an empirical approach more akin to the physical sciences.

a. Energy economics
b. Inflation
c. Opportunity cost
d. Economic

28. _____ refers to an absence of excessive fluctuations in the macroeconomy. An economy with fairly constant output growth and low and stable inflation would be considered economically stable. An economy with frequent large recessions, a pronounced business cycle, very high or variable inflation, or frequent financial crises would be considered economically unstable.
   a. Export subsidy
   b. Export-led growth
   c. Income effect
   d. Economic stability

Chapter 19. International Monetary Arrangements

1. In finance, the _____s between two currencies specifies how much one currency is worth in terms of the other. It is the value of a foreign natione;s currency in terms of the home natione;s currency. For example an _____ of 102 Japanese yen to the United States dollar means that JPY 102 is worth the same as USD 1.
   a. Interbank market
   b. Exchange rate
   c. ACEA agreement
   d. ACCRA Cost of Living Index

2. The _____ is a monetary system in which a region's common medium of exchange are paper notes that are normally freely convertible into pre-set, fixed quantities of gold. The _____ is not currently used by any government, having been replaced completely by fiat currency. Gold certificates were used as paper currency in the United States from 1882 to 1933, these certificates were freely convertable into gold coins.

   In the 1790s Britain suffered a massive shortage of silver coinage and ceased to mint larger silver coins.

   a. 100-year flood
   b. 130-30 fund
   c. 1921 recession
   d. Gold standard

3. In economics, the _____ is a term relating to the money supply, the amount of money in the economy. The _____ comprises only coins, paper money, and commercial banks' reserves with the central bank. Broader measures of the money supply include the public's bank deposits.
   a. Monetary economy
   b. Monetary base
   c. Quantum economics
   d. Chartalism

4. _____ is the process by which the government, central bank (ii) availability of money, and (iii) cost of money or rate of interest, in order to attain a set of objectives oriented towards the growth and stability of the economy. Monetary theory provides insight into how to craft optimal _____.

   _____ is referred to as either being an expansionary policy where an expansionary policy increases the total supply of money in the economy, and a contractionary policy decreases the total money supply.

   a. Monetary policy
   b. 1921 recession
   c. 100-year flood
   d. 130-30 fund

5. In economics, _____ is the total amount of money available in an economy at a particular point in time. There are several ways to define 'money', but standard measures usually include currency in circulation and demand deposits.

   _____ data are recorded and published, usually by the government or the central bank of the country.

   a. Velocity of money
   b. Neutrality of money
   c. Money supply
   d. Veil of money

6. _____ in economics and business is the result of an exchange and from that trade we assign a numerical monetary value to a good, service or asset. If Alice trades Bob 4 apples for an orange, the _____ of an orange is 4 apples. Inversely, the _____ of an apple is 1/4 oranges.
   a. Price book
   b. Price war
   c. Premium pricing
   d. Price

Chapter 19. International Monetary Arrangements

7. In economics, the _____ is one of the two primary components of the balance of payments, the other being the capital account. It is the sum of the balance of trade (exports minus imports of goods and services), net factor income (such as interest and dividends) and net transfer payments (such as foreign aid.)

$$\text{Current account} = \text{Balance of trade}$$
$$+ \text{ Net factor income from abroad}$$
$$+ \text{ Net unilateral transfers from abroad}$$

The _____ balance is one of two major metrics of the nature of a country's foreign trade (the other being the net capital outflow.)

a. National Income and Product Accounts
b. Gross private domestic investment
c. Compensation of employees
d. Current account

8. _____ is a branch of economics that deals with the performance, structure, and behavior of a national or regional economy as a whole. Along with microeconomics, _____ is one of the two most general fields in economics. It is the study of the behavior and decision-making of entire economies.

a. Tobit model
b. New Trade Theory
c. Macroeconomics
d. Nominal value

9. A _____ is a hypothetical measure of overall prices for some set of goods and services, in a given region during a given interval, normalized relative to some base set. Typically, a _____ is approximated with a price index.

The classical dichotomy is the assumption that there is a relatively clean distinction between overall increases or decreases in prices and underlying, e;reale; economic variables.

a. Discouraged worker
b. Price level
c. Price elasticity of supply
d. Discretionary spending

10. In economics, _____ is the total demand for final goods and services in the economy (Y) at a given time and price level. It is the amount of goods and services in the economy that will be purchased at all possible price levels. This is the demand for the gross domestic product of a country when inventory levels are static.

a. Aggregate demand
b. Aggregate expenditure
c. Aggregation problem
d. Aggregate supply

Chapter 19. International Monetary Arrangements

11. Economics:

    - _____, the desire to own something and the ability to pay for it
    - _____ curve, a graphic representation of a _____ schedule
    - _____ deposit, the money in checking accounts
    - _____ pull theory, the theory that inflation occurs when _____ for goods and services exceeds existing supplies
    - _____ schedule, a table that lists the quantity of a good a person will buy it each different price
    - _____ side economics, the school of economics at believes government spending and tax cuts open economy by raising _____

    a. Demand
    b. McKesson ' Robbins scandal
    c. Production
    d. Variability

12. The _____ is an international organization that oversees the global financial system by following the macroeconomic policies of its member countries, in particular those with an impact on exchange rates and the balance of payments. It is an organization formed to stabilize international exchange rates and facilitate development. It also offers financial and technical assistance to its members, making it an international lender of last resort.

    a. ACCRA Cost of Living Index
    b. International Monetary Fund
    c. ACEA agreement
    d. Office of Thrift Supervision

13. A _____, reserve bank, or monetary authority is the entity responsible for the monetary policy of a country or of a group of member states. It is a bank that can lend money to other banks in times of need. Its primary responsibility is to maintain the stability of the national currency and money supply, but more active duties include controlling subsidized-loan interest rates, and acting as a lender of last resort to the banking sector during times of financial crisis (private banks often being integral to the national financial system.)

    a. 1921 recession
    b. Central Bank
    c. 130-30 fund
    d. 100-year flood

14. The _____ is the official currency of 16 of the 27 member states of the European Union (EU.) The states, known collectively as the Eurozone, are Austria, Belgium, Cyprus, Finland, France, Germany, Greece, Ireland, Italy, Luxembourg, Malta, the Netherlands, Portugal, Slovakia, Slovenia, and Spain. The currency is also used in a further five European countries, with and without formal agreements and is consequently used daily by some 327 million Europeans.

    a. Equity capital market
    b. Import and Export Price Indices
    c. IRS Code 3401
    d. Euro

15. The _____ is one of the world's most important central banks, responsible for monetary policy covering the 16 member States of the Eurozone. It was established by the European Union (EU) in 1998 with its headquarters in Frankfurt, Germany.

    The predecessor to the _____ was the European Monetary Institute .

    a. European Central Bank
    b. ACCRA Cost of Living Index
    c. AD-IA Model
    d. ACEA agreement

Chapter 19. International Monetary Arrangements

16. _____ is sometimes referred to as _____, actually it means Economic Monetary Union.

First ideas of an economic and monetary union in Europe were raised well before establishing the European Communities. For example, already in the League of Nations, Gustav Stresemann asked in 1929 for a European currency (Link) against the background of an increased economic division due to a number of new nation states in Europe after WWI.

a. Exchange rate mechanism
b. European Monetary System
c. European Monetary Union
d. Euro Interbank Offered Rate

17. An economic and _____ is a single market with a common currency. It is to be distinguished from a mere currency union, which does not involve a single market. This is the fifth stage of economic integration.

a. Customs union
b. Commercial invoice
c. Free trade zone
d. Monetary Union

18. _____ occurs when the inhabitants of a country use foreign currency in parallel to or instead of the domestic currency.

_____ can occur

- unofficially, when private agents prefer the foreign currency over the domestic currency. They hold for example deposits in the foreign currency because of a bad track record of the local currency.

- semiofficially (or officially bimonetary systems), where foreign currency is legal tender, but plays a secondary role to domestic currency
- officially, when a country ceases to issue the domestic currency and uses only foreign currency. It adopts the foreign currency as legal tender.

The term _____ is not only applied to usage of the United States dollar, but also generally to the use of any foreign currency as the national currency.

a. Currency board
b. Commodity money
c. Dollarization
d. World currency

19. _____ describes any movement or theory that proposes a different system of supplying money and financing the economy than the current system.

_____ers may advocate any of the following, among other proposals:

- A return to the gold standard (or silver standard or bimetallism.)

- The issuance of interest-free credit from a government-controlled and fully owned central bank. These interest free but repayable loans would be used for public infrastructure and productive private investment. This proposal seeks to overcome the charge that debt-free money would cause inflation.

a. Quantum economics
c. Monetary reform
b. Silver standard
d. Fiscal theory of the price level

Chapter 20. Capital Flows and the Developing Countries

1. _____ or human capital flight is a large emigration of individuals with technical skills or knowledge, normally due to conflict, lack of opportunity, political instability, or health risks. _____ is usually regarded as an economic cost, since emigrants usually take with them the fraction of value of their training sponsored by the government. It is a parallel of capital flight which refers to the same movement of financial capital.
   - a. 130-30 fund
   - b. 1921 recession
   - c. 100-year flood
   - d. Brain drain

2. _____ is that which is owed; usually referencing assets owed, but the term can also cover moral obligations and other interactions not requiring money. In the case of assets, _____ is a means of using future purchasing power in the present before a summation has been earned. Some companies and corporations use _____ as a part of their overall corporate finance strategy.
   - a. Hard money loan
   - b. Debenture
   - c. Debt
   - d. Collateral Management

3. _____ is the concept or idea of fairness in economics, particularly as to taxation or welfare economics.

   In welfare economics, _____ may be distinguished from economic efficiency in overall evaluation of social welfare. Although '_____' has broader uses, it may be posed as a counterpart to economic inequality in yielding a 'good' distribution of welfare.

   - a. AD-IA Model
   - b. ACEA agreement
   - c. Equity
   - d. ACCRA Cost of Living Index

4. A _____ is an expression that compares quantities relative to each other. The most common examples involve two quantities, but any number of quantities can be compared. _____s are represented mathematically by separating each quantity with a colon, for example the _____ 2:3, which is read as the _____ 'two to three'.
   - a. 130-30 fund
   - b. 100-year flood
   - c. Y-intercept
   - d. Ratio

5. _____, or a _____ is the concept of a resulting effect (cf. cause and effect, arising from another action. In general terms, it is used to indicate that all human actions, particularly crime and sin, have profound effects.
   - a. Rule
   - b. Variability
   - c. Solved
   - d. Consequence

6. _____ is an economic concept that tries to explain the apparent relationship between the exploitation of natural resources and a decline in the manufacturing sector combined with moral fallout. The theory is that an increase in revenues from natural resources will deindustrialise a natione;s economy by raising the exchange rate, which makes the manufacturing sector less competitive and public services entangled with business interests. However, it is extremely difficult to definitively say that _____ is the cause of the decreasing manufacturing sector, since there are many other factors at play in the very complex global economy.
   - a. Gravity model of trade
   - b. Comparative advantage
   - c. Triffin dilemma
   - d. Dutch disease

7. _____ in economics and business is the result of an exchange and from that trade we assign a numerical monetary value to a good, service or asset. If Alice trades Bob 4 apples for an orange, the _____ of an orange is 4 apples. Inversely, the _____ of an apple is 1/4 oranges.

a. Premium pricing
c. Price book
b. Price war
d. Price

8. _____ was an American economist, statistician and public intellectual, and a recipient of the Nobel Memorial Prize in Economic Sciences. He is best known among scholars for his theoretical and empirical research, especially consumption analysis, monetary history and theory, and for his demonstration of the complexity of stabilization policy. A global public followed his restatement of a political philosophy that insisted on minimizing the role of government in favor of the private sector.
   a. Adolf Hitler
   c. Adam Smith
   b. Adolph Fischer
   d. Milton Friedman

9. The _____ is an international organization that oversees the global financial system by following the macroeconomic policies of its member countries, in particular those with an impact on exchange rates and the balance of payments. It is an organization formed to stabilize international exchange rates and facilitate development. It also offers financial and technical assistance to its members, making it an international lender of last resort.
   a. International Monetary Fund
   c. ACCRA Cost of Living Index
   b. Office of Thrift Supervision
   d. ACEA agreement

10. _____ is the prospect that a party insulated from risk may behave differently from the way it would behave if it were fully exposed to the risk. In insurance, _____ that occurs without conscious or malicious action is called morale hazard.

    _____ is related to information asymmetry, a situation in which one party in a transaction has more information than another.

    a. Moral hazard
    c. 100-year flood
    b. 1921 recession
    d. 130-30 fund

11. _____, in economics, occurs when assets and/or money rapidly flow out of a country, due to an economic event that disturbs investors and causes them to lower their valuation of the assets in that country, or otherwise to lose confidence in its economic strength. This leads to a disappearance of wealth and is usually accompanied by a sharp drop in the exchange rate of the affected country (depreciation in a variable exchange rate regime, or a forced devaluation in a fixed exchange rate regime.)

    This fall is particularly damaging when the capital belongs to the people of the affected country, because not only are the citizens now burdened by the loss of faith in the economy and devaluation of their currency, but probably also their assets have lost much of their nominal value.

    a. Capital formation
    c. Liquid capital
    b. Capital flight
    d. Firm-specific infrastructure

12. _____ refers to the transmission of a financial shock in one entity to other interdependent entities.

The study of economic contagion came to prominence in the 1990s, when a wave of currency crises affected the emerging markets around the world.

With the onset of the Subprime mortgage crisis, several countries around the world have had to deal with similar currency problems.

a. Gross regional domestic product
c. Correlation trading

b. Financial contagion
d. Concentration risk

13. _____ is a concept in international development, political economy and international relations and describes the use of conditions attached to a loan, debt relief, bilateral aid or membership of international organizations, typically by the international financial institutions, regional organizations or donor countries.

_____ is typically employed by the International Monetary Fund, the World Bank or a donor country with respect to loans, debt relief and financial aid. Conditionalities may involve relatively uncontroversial requirements to enhance aid effectiveness, such as anti-corruption measures, but they may involve highly controversial ones, such as austerity or the privatization of key public services, which may provoke strong political opposition in the recipient country.

a. Participatory rural appraisal
c. Conditionality

b. Capacity Development
d. Sector-Wide Approach

14. _____s is the social science that studies the production, distribution, and consumption of goods and services. The term _____s comes from the Ancient Greek oá¼°κονομῖα from oá¼¶κος (oikos, 'house') + vÏŒμος (nomos, 'custom' or 'law'), hence 'rules of the house(hold)'. Current _____ models developed out of the broader field of political economy in the late 19th century, owing to a desire to use an empirical approach more akin to the physical sciences.

a. Opportunity cost
c. Inflation

b. Energy economics
d. Economic

Chapter 1
1. d	2. b	3. d	4. d	5. d	6. a	7. d	8. b	9. b	10. d
11. c	12. d	13. d	14. d	15. b	16. d	17. c	18. d	19. d	20. d
21. d	22. d	23. c	24. c	25. d					

Chapter 2
1. b	2. a	3. d	4. c	5. d	6. d	7. a	8. d	9. d	10. d
11. d	12. d	13. d	14. b	15. d	16. d	17. d	18. d	19. b	20. d
21. d	22. a	23. a	24. d	25. d	26. b	27. b	28. c	29. d	30. d
31. a	32. d								

Chapter 3
1. d	2. d	3. d	4. a	5. d	6. d	7. d	8. d	9. d	10. a
11. d	12. a	13. d	14. d	15. a	16. c	17. d	18. d	19. c	20. c
21. b	22. d	23. d	24. d	25. a	26. b	27. c	28. c	29. a	30. d
31. d	32. d	33. a							

Chapter 4
1. d	2. d	3. d	4. d	5. d	6. d	7. d	8. d	9. c	10. b
11. c	12. d	13. d	14. d	15. b	16. a				

Chapter 5
1. d	2. d	3. d	4. c	5. a	6. d	7. d	8. c	9. b	10. d
11. d	12. c	13. a	14. d	15. d	16. a	17. d	18. c	19. c	20. c
21. c	22. d								

Chapter 6
1. b	2. a	3. d	4. d	5. d	6. b	7. a	8. d	9. c	10. b

Chapter 7
1. d	2. c	3. d	4. b	5. d	6. d	7. a	8. c	9. d	10. d
11. d	12. d	13. d	14. a	15. d	16. a				

Chapter 8
1. b	2. a	3. d	4. d	5. a	6. d	7. d	8. d	9. b	10. d
11. d	12. a	13. c	14. d	15. a	16. d	17. d	18. c	19. d	20. b
21. d	22. d	23. d							

Chapter 9
1. d	2. d	3. d	4. b	5. d	6. b	7. d	8. d	9. c	10. c
11. d	12. d	13. a	14. a	15. d	16. b	17. d	18. a	19. b	20. a
21. b	22. b								

ANSWER KEY

Chapter 10
1. d	2. c	3. d	4. b	5. b	6. d	7. a	8. a	9. a	10. b
11. d	12. c	13. a	14. d	15. a	16. d	17. d	18. b	19. c	20. b
21. b	22. d	23. d	24. a	25. a	26. d	27. d	28. d	29. a	

Chapter 11
1. d	2. c	3. c	4. c	5. d	6. c	7. d	8. d	9. d	10. a
11. d	12. b	13. d	14. b	15. b	16. a	17. b	18. d	19. b	20. a
21. a	22. a	23. b	24. d	25. c					

Chapter 12
1. c	2. c	3. d	4. d	5. d	6. d	7. d	8. d	9. d	10. c
11. b	12. c	13. a	14. a	15. c	16. d	17. b	18. b	19. b	20. b
21. a	22. c	23. d	24. d						

Chapter 13
1. d	2. d	3. d	4. a	5. b	6. a	7. d	8. d	9. d	10. d
11. c	12. a	13. d							

Chapter 14
1. c	2. d	3. d	4. d	5. d	6. b	7. d	8. b	9. a	10. d
11. d	12. d	13. d	14. d	15. d	16. d	17. c	18. b	19. d	20. d
21. b	22. b	23. b	24. a	25. d					

Chapter 15
1. d	2. d	3. d	4. d	5. a	6. a	7. d	8. d	9. b	10. d
11. c	12. a	13. d	14. a	15. c	16. a	17. d	18. d	19. b	20. c
21. d	22. b	23. d	24. d	25. d					

Chapter 16
1. d	2. d	3. d	4. d	5. a	6. b	7. c	8. c	9. a	10. d
11. d	12. d	13. b	14. d	15. c	16. d	17. d	18. c	19. b	20. d
21. d	22. d	23. d	24. b	25. b	26. c	27. d	28. c	29. d	30. a

Chapter 17
1. b	2. a	3. d	4. b	5. d	6. d	7. d	8. d	9. d	10. d
11. d	12. b	13. c	14. a	15. c	16. b	17. d	18. b	19. a	20. d
21. b	22. d	23. b	24. d	25. d	26. d	27. c	28. d	29. d	

Chapter 18
1. a	2. b	3. a	4. d	5. d	6. d	7. d	8. d	9. c	10. d
11. d	12. c	13. d	14. a	15. d	16. d	17. d	18. d	19. a	20. d
21. b	22. a	23. d	24. d	25. d	26. d	27. d	28. d		

Chapter 19
1. b 2. d 3. b 4. a 5. c 6. d 7. d 8. c 9. b 10. a
11. a 12. b 13. b 14. d 15. a 16. c 17. d 18. c 19. c

Chapter 20
1. d 2. c 3. c 4. d 5. d 6. d 7. d 8. d 9. a 10. a
11. b 12. b 13. c 14. d